THE JOHN DEWEY LECTURE

The John Dewey Lecture has been delivered annually since 1958 under the sponsorship of the John Dewey Society. The intention of the series is to provide a setting where able thinkers from various sectors of our intellectual life can direct their most searching thoughts to problems that involve the relation of education to culture. Arrangements for the presentation of the Lecture and its publication by Teachers College Press are under the direction of Daniel Tanner, Chairperson.

RECENT TITLES IN THE SERIES

Excellence in Public Discourse:
John Stuart Mill, John Dewey, and Social Intelligence
James Gouinlock

Building a Global Civic Culture:
Education for an Interdependent World
Elise Boulding

The Dialectic of Freedom
Maxine Greene

Education for Intelligent Belief or Unbelief
Nel Noddings

Cultural Politics and Education
Michael W. Apple

In Praise of Education
John I. Goodlad

John Dewey and the Philosopher's Task
Philip W. Jackson

John Dewey
and the
Philosopher's Task

Philip W. Jackson

TEACHERS
COLLEGE
PRESS

Teachers College, Columbia University
New York and London

Published by Teachers College Press, 1234 Amsterdam Avenue, New York, NY 10027

Author's note: The author wishes to express gratitude for the use of material excerpted from the following:

The Collected Works of John Dewey: Later Works (*Volumes 1, 5,* and *14*). Edited by Jo Ann Boydston, and © 1981, 1984, and 1988, respectively, by the Board of Trustees, Southern Illinois University. Reprinted by permission.

The Poems of John Dewey. Edited by Jo Ann Boydston, and © 1977 by Southern Illinois University Press. Reprinted by permission.

Library of Congress Cataloging-in-Publication Data

Jackson, Philip W. (Philip Wesley), 1928-
    John Dewey and the philosopher's task / Philip W. Jackson.
       p. cm. — (The John Dewey lecture)
    Includes bibliographical references and index.
    ISBN 0-8077-4165-5 (pbk. : alk. paper) — ISBN 0-8077-4166-3 (cloth: alk. paper)
    1. Dewey, John, 1859–1952. I. Title. II. John Dewey lecture (Teachers College Press)
    B945.D44 J33 2001
    191—dc2l   2001044598

ISBN 0-8077-4165-5 (paper)
ISBN 0-8077-4166-3 (cloth)

Printed on acid-free paper

Manufactured in the United States of America

09 08 07 06 05 04 03 02   8 7 6 5 4 3 2 1

In Memory of
Ida May and Ray Hoffman

Things that really matter, although they are not defined for all eternity, even when they come very late still come at the right time.

—Martin Heidegger, *Pathmarks*, 262

Contents

Foreword

Philip Jackson has, once again, given us a penetrating analysis of John Dewey at work. I say, "at work" because the brilliance of Jackson's book is the disclosure of two features at once. The first is Dewey's personal struggle with a knotty philosophical question that continues to haunt philosophy. The other is Jackson's own struggle with Dewey.

Dewey wrestled with two major competing views of reality, one rooted in what Jackson calls, "absolute empiricism," and the other, in "absolute idealism." The former argues that the only thing that can be known is situated in the world we experience *directly*. The competing view argues that the only things that we can know are the ideas that we ourselves make. As a philosopher who eschewed dichotomies of this sort and of others, Dewey was not prone to accept this either-or.

What we find in Jackson's book is a story of Dewey's travels both intellectually and emotionally as he attempted to make himself plain to readers on this deep philosophical matter, a journey whose direction was often far from clear. In this sense, what we secure from Jackson's narrative is a story of a struggle, one revealed in Dewey's efforts to revise the introduction to one of his most important books, *Experience and Nature*. It is a struggle guided by a conviction that philosophers ought not be concerned with nailing down either the facts or some final truth, but to be concerned with progress step by step: philosophical understanding proceeds haltingly. Philosophy, according to Dewey, is a pursuit not a destination. The quest for certainty, the title of one of his books published in 1927, is hopeless.

This Deweyan disposition gives a central place to inquiry. In a sense, Dewey believed that though it was all that we had, this approach was far from infallible. What we get from Jackson is a revelation of Dewey's struggles, a revelation that emerges more vividly in the poetry that Dewey wrote (some of which Jackson includes here) than in his philosophical writing. It was in his poetic moments, according to Jackson, that the emotional side of Dewey was most clearly revealed. His persona as a philosopher displays the cool demeanor of a thinker whose passion and ire are displayed only from time to time and largely in his reaction to work in philosophy that he believed wrong-headed. Poetry, in a sense, was liberating. It gave him permission to be in the world in ways other than those that philosophy made possible.

But Jackson does more than inform us about the struggles Dewey was having with a deep philosophical question. Jackson gives us access to his own struggles with Dewey. What we find as we read Jackson's book is a display of uncertainties, puzzlements, quandaries, conjectures. Thus, in a very interesting way, Dewey's uncertainties about the resolution of a basic philosophical issue are echoed in Jackson's attempt to disrobe Dewey.

Jackson says practically nothing about education, yet the moral of the story, if I can express it this way, is fundamentally educational. It is a display of the quest to understand what Dewey pursued throughout his life, and it is an example of Jackson's pursuit to understand the grounds of Dewey's quest. It is in this sense that *John Dewey and The Philosopher's Task* is profoundly educational. It is not educational as Jackson might say, "in the hard sense," but it is certainly educational in the soft sense.

Dewey believed that neither philosophy nor science had a method of inquiry in the hard sense; there were no strict procedures, no algorithms, no steps to be taken that could be routinely, and one might say mindlessly, applied in order to get to a goal. Philosophy and science required much more than that. But there was a method in the soft sense: the need to reason, to exercise judgment, to see "from afar," to consider alternatives, to be open to criticism. Put another way, both philosophy and science are creative enterprises that do not submit to routines. One does them with all of one's humanity.

Such a view of philosophy and science can also, when broadened, be applied to education. Indeed, it could be applied to education as an ideal that teachers and schools as institutions might consider emulating. It could become an ideal that could shape the culture of the school and therefore the processes of teaching and learning. Thus, Jackson has indeed given us a book on education. He leaves it to us to read not only the lines, but the spaces between them to find, in an age that seeks relentlessly to achieve predictable outcomes measured by new technology, another vision, one guided by the humanistic values and the perspectives that Dewey increasingly embraced as he matured. There are, after all, tasks implied here not only for philosophers, but also for those of us who care about education.

Elliot W. Eisner
Stanford University

Acknowledgments

This book began as one of the annual John Dewey Lectures sponsored by the John Dewey Society. I am grateful to Elliot Eisner, then President of the Society, and to members of its selection committee, for inviting me to deliver that lecture.

David Hansen read a draft of the full manuscript and offered many helpful suggestions for its improvement. His insightful reading led to a number of changes that clearly strengthened the book as a whole. I am indebted to him for that help and accept sole responsibility for whatever weaknesses remain.

My wife, Jo, patiently listened to me read portions of the manuscript aloud to her during its preparation. Her critical reactions on those occasions were, as always, immensely valuable and much appreciated.

As she has done for me in the past, Carole Saltz, Director of Teachers College Press, was quick to give her warm support to my work on this project. I much appreciate her steadfast interest in seeing it to completion. Susan Liddicoat, my able editor at the Press, helped immensely in giving final shape to the submitted manuscript. Her detailed editorial suggestions made the task far less burdensome than it might otherwise have been. Jonas Soltis, who allowed himself to be identified as the anonymous reader to whom the Press had turned for an outside opinion, was exceedingly forthright and succinct in his commentary. I could not have hoped for a more highly respected evaluator or a more generous evaluation.

Introduction

If we find those who are engaged in metaphysical pursuits, unable to come to an understanding as to the method which they ought to follow; if we find them, after the most elaborate preparations, invariably brought to a stand before the goal is reached, and compelled to retrace their steps and strike into fresh paths, we may then feel quite sure that they are far from having attained to the certainty of scientific progress and may rather be said to be merely groping about in the dark.

—Immanuel Kant, *The Critique of Pure Reason,* 1952, 5

Think not the torch
Is one of joy and light.
Its scatter'd sparks but scorch
And die in falling night.
. . .
No course is lit
By light that former burned
From darkness bit by bit
The present road is learned.

—John Dewey, *The Poems of John Dewey,* 1977, 64–65

John Dewey was not a scientist, though he respected the goal of scientific progress fully as much as did Kant. Neither was he a poet, though he dabbled at the craft from time to time, as the above lines attest. Like Kant, he was basically a philosopher, arguably the finest this nation has yet produced. He was certainly among its most prolific.

Among the many topics that philosophers address one stands out as being a near favorite. That topic is philosophy itself. Philosophers are understandably interested in its future. They ponder its mission. They fret about its standing in the public eye. They consider its place in human affairs. They think about how it should be practiced.

This book is about an extended concatenation of Dewey's thoughts on what he called "philosophic method." It began by my puzzling over the odd history of his repeated attempts to introduce *Experience and Nature*, one of his best known works—some would say his *magnum opus*—to successive audiences of new readers. That history unfolds as follows:

The first edition of *Experience and Nature* appeared in 1925 to widespread critical acclaim. The vast majority of reviewers (more than twenty-five in the year of its publication) hailed it as a major work by America's preeminent living philosopher. Even those who had something critical to say did so respectfully. Dewey can only have been pleased with the book's overall reception and with the high praise it garnered.

Yet his pleasure must have been diminished somewhat by his own critical judgment of one crucial segment of the book—its opening chapter. Dewey had to agree with the unfavorable remarks of a few of his readers. As he subsequently confessed in the first revised edition of the work, that initial chapter, entitled "Experience and Philosophic Method," "was upon the whole more technical and harder reading than the chapters which it was supposed to introduce." Nor was that all. "It was also rather confused," Dewey acknowledged. The confusion, he said, was "in mode of presentation and at one important point in thought as well" (LW1, 3).[1]

In 1929, when the book was being prepared for its third impression, Dewey undertook to correct those initial shortcomings. His remedy was radical. Instead of simply revising what he had written at the start, leaving large parts of it unchanged, he cast aside the original first chapter and replaced it with a new version. He also added a Preface designed to give an overview of the book and explain how its ten chapters related to one another. The 1929 revised edition with its completely rewritten first chapter and its new Preface has over the years become the standard version of the work. It is the one most readily available to today's readers.[2]

Almost two decades pass before our tale picks up again. In 1948, after finishing an Introduction to a reissue of *Reconstruction in Philosophy*, another book written in the twenties, Dewey turned to the task of writing a similar introduction for a planned reissue of *Experience and Nature*. The draft manuscript that grew out of that effort bore the title "Experience and Nature: A Re-Introduction."

Reissued books by living authors customarily begin with a statement about how the book in question holds up in the light of social and intellectual changes that have taken place since its initial publication. The typescript of the book itself, however, is seldom changed. Dewey, it seems, planned to follow that custom.

His work on the Re-Introduction yielded a sizeable document, which was subsequently worked on editorially by Joseph Ratner, a fellow philosopher and colleague at Columbia University who helped to edit Dewey's postwar writings. The version of that Re-Introduction that appears in Dewey's *Collected Works* runs to thirty printed pages, which is slightly longer than the initial (1925) chapter and only one page shy of the length of the second (1929) version. Moreover, Dewey apparently intended it to be even longer, for its final section ends abruptly, as though the author clearly had more to say.

Unfortunately, other commitments plus a lingering illness forced Dewey to lay that project aside for a time. How that unfinished manuscript, begun in 1948, might have ended we unfortunately will never know. When Dewey returned to the task in 1951, more than two years later, he did not simply take up where he had left off, as one might have expected him to do, but instead put aside what he had written, inserted a clean sheet of paper into his typewriter, and began afresh, just as he had done with the revised first chapter in 1929. Moreover, his fresh beginning is enough to make everyone who is acquainted with Dewey's work as a whole sit up and take notice. It begins with: "Were I to write (or rewrite) *Experience and Nature* today I would entitle the book *Culture and Nature*" (LW1, 361). Given the prominence afforded the concept of experience throughout Dewey's writings, that opening remark comes as quite a surprise. Dewey's editor, Joseph Ratner, was sufficiently impressed by it to declare that in considering such a change Dewey was, in effect, transforming "the task of finishing the Introduction into a formidable new problem" (LW1, 361).

As fate would have it, Dewey did not live to deliver on that promise. He was then ninety-two and was destined to die within the year. Like the unfinished manuscript that had preceded it, his fourth and final effort to introduce—actually to re-introduce—*Experience and Nature* ended abruptly, almost in mid-sentence. A scant eight paragraphs (six pages in print) were all he managed to complete.

Thus ends the brief account of the events that so puzzled me at the start. Why, I wondered, did Dewey find the task of introducing *Experience and Nature* sufficiently challenging to take it up on four separate occasions? More important, why was he dissatisfied, or seemingly so, with each successive attempt?

My initial hunch, no more than a wild guess I must confess, was that in his four attempts Dewey was trying to say something very important but for some reason failing to get it right. Was he, I wondered, getting closer and closer to his goal each time around?

That kind of conjecturing about what might have been going on within Dewey's mind was enough to set me to work examining with care the four introductory statements, comparing each with the others. As a result of that comparison, I did manage to discern (or thought I did) something like an apparent direction in which Dewey's successive attempts were headed. The conclusions I came to, along with the course I took in getting there, are laid out in detail in the chapters to follow.

What I also came to realize along the way, aided greatly by a book by John Shook (2000) that I chanced to read when I was quite far along in my work,[3] was that the unknown "something" that I had initially imagined Dewey to have been pursuing was not the "formidable new problem" to which Ratner saw him headed near the close of his life. Instead it was a formidable *old* problem, one that Dewey had been pondering since the start of his professional career. At the heart of that problem, as has already been suggested, lies the question of how philosophers should go about their work. I further came to see that Dewey's continued exploration of that question, a portion of which shows up in his efforts to introduce *Experience and Nature* to its various audiences, is not best looked upon as consisting of a series of successive attempts to get something right, to nail it down once and for all. It is better seen, as I hope subsequently to make clear, as part of a lifelong effort to translate into both words and action that complicated cluster of ideals, hopes, and aversions that form the core of Dewey's philosophy. I expand upon that notion at the close of this volume.

It should be evident from what has been said so far, as well as from my way of saying it, that this book is not written for professional philosophers, at least not primarily. Its primary audience, as I envision it, consists of readers, like me, who are sufficiently interested in philosophy in general and in the writings of Dewey in particular to want to know more about his final efforts to address the all-important question of the relationship between philosophy and human affairs.[4]

I write not as a specialist in philosophy but as someone who has studied and admired Dewey's writings for many years. I trust that what I have to say will be received as coming from such a source rather than from a professional exegete of philosophical texts. I have felt from the start that Dewey would have approved of what I was trying to do, even though he might have disagreed with some of my judgments. I picture him as welcoming commentary from all quarters and not from experts alone, not even if that being commented upon was initially written for a rather exclusive and specialized audience—as was certainly true of *Experience and Nature*.[5] I trust that most of my readers will agree with my presumption about how Dewey might have responded to my effort and will themselves react similarly.

The plan of the book is as follows: Chapters 1 and 2 are devoted, respectively, to the two published versions of Chapter 1 of *Experience and Nature*. Chapter 3 treats the two unpublished introductions prepared for the book's reissue. Chapter 4 explores the figurative nature of Dewey's conception of the philosopher's task. Chapter 5 returns to the key idea of philosophic method. Throughout all five chapters some repetition is unavoidable, as the main point of the exercise is to see how Dewey modifies or fails to modify his conception of the philosopher's task as he moves from one version of the introductory material to the next. An Afterword containing some personal reflections on the entire project brings the volume to a close.

John Dewey
and the
Philosopher's Task

CHAPTER 1

The Initial First Chapter (1925)

I had [heard] it said by my well-wishers that I lacked experience. . . . I had occasionally importuned my friend Behrisch to make clear to me what experience might be. Full of nonsense as he was, he put me off from one day to the next and finally, after many preliminaries, disclosed the following: true experience, in the last analysis, is when one experiences how an experienced person, while experiencing, must experience experience. When we scolded him severely for this and called him to account, he asserted that a great secret lay behind these words, which we would only grasp when we had experienced [he could go on like this for fifteen minutes at a time] since then experiencing would become ever more experienced and eventually a true experience. When we were near to being driven to desperation by these jokes, he protested that he had learned this manner of making himself clear and effective from our newest and greatest authors.

—Johann Wolfgang von Goethe, *From My Life:*
Poetry and Truth, 1987, 230

THE CHAPTER'S THREE OPENING PARAGRAPHS

As has already been pointed out, the original (1925) first chapter of *Experience and Nature* was entitled "Experience and Philosophic Method."[1] It begins with Dewey's complaining about the "slipperiness" of the word *experience.* It was that complaint that brought to mind Goethe's report of the comments of his friend Behrisch, who also found the word a bit slippery. Dewey, however, quite unlike Behrisch, is in no joking mood when he speaks of its slipperiness, a difference that will soon be apparent. He quotes with approval Ralph Barton Perry of Harvard who had called experience "a weasel word." As Dewey explains,

> Its slipperiness is evident in an inconsistency characteristic of many thinkers. On the one hand they eagerly claim an empirical method; they forswear the

a priori and transcendent; they are sensitive to the charge that they employ data unwarranted by experience. On the other hand, they are given to deprecating the conception of experience; experience, it is said, is purely subjective, and whoever takes experience for his subject-matter is logically bound to land in the most secluded of idealisms (LW1, 365).

Dewey does not say who these "many thinkers" are that he has in mind, but the ease with which he proceeds to describe them suggests that his readers would have no trouble recognizing them. I presume Dewey used the inclusive phrase "many thinkers" because he wanted it to cover more than just philosophers. One can easily imagine certain psychologists of the day and perhaps even some physical scientists fitting the description he gives. Whoever they may be, their distinguishing characteristic is that they put their trust in experience when it is looked upon in one way (i.e., empirically) but distrust it when looked upon in another way (i.e., psychologically).

How do people come to exhibit such inconsistency? Again, Dewey does not say. He does, however, offer a partial explanation.

It may be surmised, however, that those guilty of the contradiction think in two insulated universes of discourse. In adherence to empirical method, they think of experience in terms of the modern development of scientific method; but their idea of experience as a distinctive subject matter is derived from another source—introspective psychology as it was elaborated in the nineteenth century (LW1, 365).

Regardless of the origin of such contradictory ways of thinking, Dewey calls for their prompt abandonment. "We must," he says, "make a choice," which he elaborates as follows:

If the identification of experience with purely mental states is correct, then the last thing one should profess is acceptance of empirical method as the scientific road to the understanding of the natural and social world in which we live. And if scientific method is intrinsically empirical, then the subject-matter of experience cannot be what introspective psychologists have told us it is (LW1, 365).

Given the stress Dewey has placed on this proffered choice, we must of course look closely at its terms. Before doing so, however, I must add one more quotation to those already presented. The rather lengthy paragraph that follows the words quoted above rounds off

Dewey's preamble to the topic he treats in the remainder of the chapter. Here it is in full.

> Whether or not this suggestion is correct, recognition of the inconsistency is of use in enabling us, writer and reader alike, to trap and hold the slippery idea of experience, whenever it is proposed to set forth the implications of experience for philosophy; especially when, as in this discussion, its implications for a theory of nature, of the world, of the universe, form the issue. And I know of no better way of warning the reader against misconception of this purpose than to remind him that, as he reads the statement, he should interpret "experience" in the sense in which he himself uses the term when he professes to be faithful to the empirical method, not in the sense in which he uses it when he implies that experience is momentary, private and psychical (LW1, 366).

Commentary

These three introductory paragraphs invite so many comments that it is hard to know where to begin. Perhaps the first thing to note is that they alone provide ample reason for Dewey's wanting to revise the first chapter. They do indeed comprise a difficult beginning of his book (whether more difficult than later sections or than the revised chapter that we soon enough examine are questions that need not concern us here). I confess that I find them more than a bit confusing. This is not to say that Dewey was himself confused about what he was trying to say (although he might have been), but it is certainly evident (at least to me) that he was not saying whatever it was he wanted to say as clearly as he might have.

What I propose to do, therefore, is to share my own sense of puzzlement as it emerged for me during my reading of the text. I will at the same time indicate what I believe Dewey meant to say or might have said if queried further about each of the points raised. My suppositions about what Dewey intended to say or might have said are based on things he says elsewhere, either in this text or in other of his writings.

I begin with Dewey's complaint about the slipperiness of the word *experience*. It is certainly the case that the word is used in the two senses that Dewey notes. No one can dispute that. But is that ample reason for calling the word slippery? Do those different usages ordinarily create confusion? I think not. And I do not believe that Dewey thinks so either. What then is the problem? Why is he upset?

What upsets him, as I see it, has little to do with language per se, at least not in any narrow sense. Dewey is not out to legislate anyone's speech habits. On the contrary, he elsewhere appears quite content with our ordinary ways of speaking.

Dewey's unease has to do with the way "many thinkers," which I take to include not only philosophers but also other intellectuals (principally, perhaps, certain nineteenth-century psychologists), think about experience or behave toward it. And how is that? What is their way and why does Dewey see it as being misguided?

They think (or behave), he says, as though they inhabited "two insulated universes of discourse." But what does that mean? What is a universe of discourse? And how does one think in two of them? Indeed, isn't the phrase itself inherently contradictory? If there are two of them, how can either one be universal? Much here calls for clarification.

Let us first try to get straight what Dewey sees as being the defining characteristics of each of these "two universes of discourse." To avoid worrying about whether universes can come in pairs I will stick with the more prosaic expression: two ways of thinking about experience. The first of them looks upon the word *experience* as a term that refers to what goes on whenever a living creature interacts with its environment (let us for the present simplify things by limiting such creatures to human beings). We use the word in this way when we ask someone, "Do you have any sales experience?" or when we say, "She is an experienced plumber." Dewey wants to call this the empirical conception of experience. It is the conception that scientists (and others) supposedly employ whenever they claim to be using an empirical method. Holders of this view also commonly eschew what Dewey calls "the *a priori* and transcendental," notions that allegedly acknowledge existences that fall outside of experience in one way or another. Dewey, I take it, has no fundamental discomfort with this way of using the term.

The other way of conceptualizing experience is by using the term to refer to what goes on within one's field of consciousness. This is the way we employ it when we ask someone, "What are you now experiencing?" or when someone says, "What an experience that was!" Dewey wants to call this the subjective or psychological conception of experience. It is this conception, Dewey tells us, that was made central and elaborated by the so-called introspective psychologists of the nineteenth century.

Now the interesting point is that Dewey has no objection to this conception of experience either. He has no interest in denying the reality of our so-called inner life. In fact, he celebrates it. What then is the problem?

The problem, it seems, is that some people (many, we are told) want to look upon the subjective aspect of experience in two ways at once. They acknowledge subjectivity to be essential, as they must if they are to be empirical, for how can one deal with the world of physical objects without having subjective ideas about them or subjective purposes to fulfill? But *at the same time*, or in some sort of parallel space and time (by entering some other "universe of discourse"?), they want to deprecate all of that "subjective stuff," especially when it is held up to inspection, that is, when it is treated as subject matter in its own right. They then not only deprecate the subjective but proceed to deny its existence. Why so? Because they see it as a threat. They see it as leading them somewhere they do not want to go.

Dewey alludes to this attraction in the third and final sentence of his opening paragraph. He says that such "thinkers" are "given" (i.e., naturally inclined?) to deprecate such a conception of experience because they see it as "logically bound" to land them "in the most secluded of idealisms." What is the most secluded of idealisms? It is what philosophers call "absolute idealism," wherein nothing is said to have any existence beyond "spirit" or consciousness itself.

The spectre of extreme psychological seclusion is encapsulated in the single word *purely*, which Dewey uses twice in the first two paragraphs of his introduction. He talks about experience being looked upon as "*purely* subjective" and about its "identification" with "*purely* mental states." It is then, presumably, that empiricism has been abandoned and a contradictory set of assumptions adopted.

It is worth noting that Dewey is not finding fault with idealism per se. He is only objecting to those who feel drawn by logic toward the most extreme (i.e., "most secluded") form of idealism once they have taken the step of acknowledging the distinctiveness of the subjective aspect of experience. It is as though they were saying to themselves: "One must be cautious about looking upon ideas and other subjective states as being real, because once one does, one stands in danger of being driven by logic to deny the reality of everything else— that is, of becoming an absolute "idealist." The remedy is to deprecate experience as purely subjective but to do so without abandoning our reliance on subjective states as they are woven within and among the actions that comprise the empirical method. Thus emerges the constellation of attitudes that Dewey calls contradictory. Such individuals want to have their cake and eat it too. They are perfectly willing to acknowledge the subjective aspects of their own commerce with the environment—the crucial importance of their own ideas, purposes, plans, and so forth—yet they remain suspect of the subjective when it is treated as an isolated set of phenomena.

How does Dewey recommend we escape this predicament? By making a choice. But a choice between what and what? This question returns us to his two if–then statements that we previously passed over quickly, too quickly, I fear. I will restate each of them, followed by a paraphrase and commentary. The first says:

> If the identification of experience with purely mental states is correct, then the last thing one should profess is acceptance of empirical method as the scientific road to the understanding of the natural and social world in which we live (LWI, 365).

What this says is that if absolute idealism is correct, if, that is, there is nothing to experience save subjective conditions (purely mental states), then an empirical (scientific) method, whereby the organism supposedly has direct physical contact with an outside world, makes no sense at all.

But this is precisely what the professed empiricist already contends, which is why she rejects absolute idealism and deprecates subjectivity as subject matter for fear of its offering the royal road to precisely that most secluded end.

The second says:

> And if scientific method is intrinsically empirical, then the subject-matter of experience cannot be what introspective psychologists have told us it is (LW1, 365).

This says that if the scientific method *requires* the possibility of direct exchange with a world outside the organism, which empiricists know it to do, then the subject matter of experience cannot be limited exclusively to what goes on within the organism—that is, to what is *purely* subjective—as certain introspective psychologists have apparently proposed.

But this too is what the professed empiricist already believes. So where is the choice? Something is missing.

What I think Dewey is calling for at one level is the forthright choice of the empirical method and a corresponding rejection of absolute idealism and of notions leading up to it. But this call is becoming tangled with another of Dewey's pleas which is to encourage committed empiricists, who by fiat have thereby explicitly rejected the possibility of absolute idealism, to stop deprecating the subjective in a way that closes the door to other, less extreme forms of idealism. Another way of putting it might be to say that he is tacitly pleading for committed empiricists in their rejection of absolute idealism to avoid moving in the direction of absolute realism. However, that second way of putting it moves us far ahead of the story, since Dewey does not here mention the rejection of absolute realism and there is some question of whether he could have done so at this historical moment.[2]

Dewey clearly lacks confidence in the alternatives he has put forth. For he quickly says, "Whether or no this suggestion is correct," and then goes on to suggest that the recognition of the inconsistency he has brought to light is nonetheless useful in enabling "writer and reader alike, to trap and hold the slippery idea of experience, whenever it is proposed to set forth the implications of experience for philosophy" (LW1, 365). It is worth noting that Dewey includes himself as "writer" among those who stand to benefit by recogizing the possibility of inconsistency of belief. I take this to mean that Dewey himself is not immune to the temptations that lead others to believe two universes of discourse exist and thus become confused. He returns finally to the notion of experience itself as slippery, hard to hold on to. He leaves his readers unclear, however, about what makes it so.

We are now only three paragraphs along in our close examination of Dewey's original first chapter of *Experience and Nature*. At this pace our analysis would go on forever, so we must hasten along. However, the problem that I sense Dewey wrestling with in these opening paragraphs is so crucial to an understanding of his book as a whole and so closely tied to the subsequent revisions he undertook that I must delay just a bit longer in order to amplify on what Dewey has said so far.

The problem, in a nutshell, is how to avoid the lures of absolute idealism on the one hand and absolute realism on the other while remaining philosophical in orientation and empirical in method. Remaining philosophical in orientation requires, according to philosophy's tradition, theorizing about (reflecting upon) human and nonhuman affairs at the very highest levels of abstraction. Remaining empirical in method means staying within the confines of experience even while theorizing, not as a matter of choice but simply because there is no alternative. I thus believe that Dewey's call for a choice in such matters is misleading. For, as he makes clear in other contexts, he believes that those who think they have somehow escaped the confines of experience and have established a beachhead of certainty in either absolute realism or absolute idealism have actually committed *the* philosophical fallacy.

The dynamics leading up to such a fallacy may be summarized as follows. In our ordinary commerce with the world, and even in the way scientists normally interact with it, the distinction between the physical and the psychological, the objective and the subjective aspects of experience, is not continually of uppermost importance. In fact, we may remain unmindful of such distinctions much of the time. When we do pay them heed, however, as we must on occasion and as philosophers are wont to do almost by habit, the temptation arises to remark upon such differences and to say something about the relative importance or even the reality of each side of the dichotomy. Such natural proclivities toward extremism elevate one side of that dichotomy to primacy and ultimately to exclusivity over the other. Thus are born absolute realists on the one side and absolute idealists on the other.[3]

Dewey will have no truck with either extreme. His writings in general make that clear. But on this particular occasion his attention appears to be focused on the attractions of absolute idealism and on the aversion to subjectivity in general that such an attraction generates among otherwise committed empiricists. Thus perhaps inadvertently he falls into talk about the existence of a "choice" when there is none to be made.

THE CHAPTER'S CENTRAL TOPIC

Having attended to Dewey's opening paragraphs in considerable detail, we are at last ready to move on to what he sees as the central topic of this introductory chapter. At issue, he says, are "the implications of experience for philosophy . . . its implication for a theory of nature, of the world, of the universe" (LW1, 366). Note the scope and the ambition of the theorizing Dewey assigns to philosophy. Also note its empirical focus. There is not the slightest hint that philosophy has to do with anything supernatural or other-worldly. Its province lies firmly within the realm of experience. But what is a theory of nature, the world, the universe? What would one look like? And how would one get started on such a task? At this point Dewey offers only the hint of an answer to the second of those questions.

He does so by outlining another choice that faces those philosophers committed to a wholehearted empiricism. They must choose one of two starting places. Either they may begin their philosophic investigations within the realm of ordinary experience, "experience in gross, experience in its primary and crude forms," or they may choose to start with the refined and sophisticated products of science (LW1, 366).

These two "methods," as Dewey calls them, differ both in their "starting point" and their "direction," yet, oddly enough, they remain identical in "objective or eventual content." This is so, Dewey explains, because those who take the scientific route must still "somehow journey back to the homely facts of daily existence," whereas those who start from those "homely facts" must also return there in the end (LW1, 366). Thus, though they both wind up at the same spot, mulling over the same "eventual content"—that is, the stuff of ordinary, everyday experience—they have traversed different routes in getting there.[4]

The initial question, once again, is where the philosopher is to begin—with ordinary experience or with the refined products of science? For Dewey, the choice is easy. He picks ordinary experience, leaving the path of science to others. He does so, he explains, partly because he lacks the technical know-how that would enable him to take the other route. Those who possess that knowledge he calls "fortunate."

It is well to keep in mind that in the mid-twenties, at just about the time when Dewey was offering this explanation for his own choice of a philosophical starting place, many of the most prominent philosophers in both Europe and America were moving or had already moved in quite the opposite direction. By the time Dewey retired from academic life those who had made the "scientific" choice had become philosophy's vanguard.[5]

Whatever feelings of envy or regret Dewey may have had as a result of his own lack of technical preparedness, the latter was by no means his only reason for choosing as he did. The scientific path, Dewey's "road not taken," has its pitfalls as well as its attractions, which Dewey proceeds to point out.

Philosophers who select that route often "get lost on a bypath." They do so, he explains, by taking "science to be something finished, absolute in itself, instead of the result of a certain technique" (LW1, 366). As a result, scientifically inclined philosophers tend to elevate the scientific findings of their own time and place to the status of philosophical premises—that is, suppositions and assumptions no longer open to empirical test—instead of looking upon them as provisional reports containing only the most secure knowledge available to date. In the process of doing so they tend to "deny, discount or pervert the obvious and immediate facts of gross experience" in favor of the facts provided by science. When that happens, Dewey concludes, "philosophy itself commits suicide" (LW1, 366).

A stronger indictment than the one contained in that series of warnings is hard to imagine. Notice what binds those warnings together. It is the flawed belief or conviction that science somehow succeeds in reaching a truth that lies beyond experience, a truth no longer open to empirical test. Dewey signals its closure to further inspection with the words "finished, absolute." Absolute truth stands in contrast to the "obvious and immediate facts" (the particular "truths," as one might say) of gross experience, which, Dewey warns, are not to be denied or discounted. But why does the elevation of scientific findings to the status of absolute truth, conjoined with the denial of the facts of gross experience, spell philosophy's suicide?

It does so, Dewey believed, because a philosophy in pursuit of absolute truth is no longer an empirical endeavor, if it ever was one. It is a project with its ultimate end in sight. All that remains is a filling in of the blanks through a dialectical process of ratiocination. That process may take some time to complete, true enough, but that it has a rational terminus remains uncontested once the first brick of certainty has been tapped into place.[6]

The Drawbacks of Starting With Ordinary Experience

As much as Dewey favors beginning one's philosophical meanderings within the province of ordinary experience, he acknowledges drawbacks associated with that approach as well. He warns that such a beginning requires "unusual candor and patience" (LW1, 367). It does so, presumably, because "coarse and vital" experience, which he now contrasts with the "definite body of facts and principles" that make up the subject matter of science, is "Protean; a thing of moods and tenses." "To seize and report it," he goes on, "is the task of an artist as well as of an informed technician" (LW1, 367).

One of the things that calls for candor, presumably, is the acknowledgment of the choices the philosopher makes in selecting a particular starting place. Dewey notes that many who call themselves *empiricists* are the worst offenders in this regard. They substitute dialectical development of some notion about experience [based chiefly on the utterances of other "advanced" thinkers] for an analysis of experience as it is humanly lived (LWI, 368).

What makes that move ironic is the fact that these nominal empiricists often become convinced that they are moving "nearer to the reality of experience the further away [they] get from all the experience [they] have ever had!" (LW1, 368).

The need for patience arises presumably because of the sheer variety of ordinary experience, which is surely enough to bewilder and confuse those looking for a place to start. As Dewey acknowledges a little further on,

> The objection is that experience is then made so inclusive and varied as to be useless for philosophic purposes. Experience, as we are here told to conceive it, includes just everything and anything, actual or potential, that we think of and talk about. So we might just as well start with everything and anything and drop out the idea and word, "experience" (LW1, 371).

Another Place to Start: Forms of Experience.

How is the philosopher to take hold of such a vast and amorphous subject matter? Dewey does not address that question directly at the start. He does, however, drop a hint about how to proceed. As early as the fourth paragraph of the chapter he says, "We may begin with experience in gross, experience in its primary and crude forms" (LW1, 366).

The hint lies in the word *forms*. That word tells us that "experience in gross," which seemingly covers everything and anything, as Dewey elsewhere points out, is not an amorphous mass. It has structure. It comes *prepackaged*, so to speak, though not perhaps as neatly as is true of the subject matter of the sciences. It comes in *forms*, primary and crude though they may be. This means, as Dewey gets around to saying some ten pages later,

> A thinker [who wants to begin with common experience] . . . finds . . . that as an empiricist he is not obliged to face the miscellaneous world *en masse*. Things are pointed to in kinds, possessed of order and arrangement. Prephilosophic selections and arrangings may not be final for reflective thought, but they are significant for it (LW1, 375).

In other words, the preexisting forms of gross experience establish crudely defined limits within which the philosopher may choose to work. Dewey calls such choices "pre-philosophic selections." He also refers to them as "adjectival groupings of macroscopic experience" (LW1, 377). The limits they establish are by no means firmly set. They may be challenged or altered as the investigation proceeds. They do, however, circumscribe an initial *field* of investigation, a place to dig in.

What are some of the forms that gross experience takes? Dewey answers,

> The key . . . is found in the adjectives that are commonly prefixed to experience. Experience is political, religious, esthetic, industrial, intellectual, mine, yours.

Philosophy, he adds, "is a branch of that . . . [type of experience] which is qualified by the adjective 'intellectual'" (LW1, 375).

As a subtype of intellectual experience philosophy does not become its own distinctive subject matter, since philosophers need not concern themselves exclusively with matters pertaining to philosophy's past or with reflections on its present and future. It is hard to imagine them completely ignoring such subject matter, however, while still referring to what they are doing as philosophy. Thus, in a sense philosophers do have a kind of obligatory subject matter even though it may be neither distinctively nor exclusively theirs. *Experience and Nature* is, in a manner of speaking, Dewey's treatment of that obligatory subject matter.

Toward the end of the first chapter, Dewey repeats his point about experience as subdivided into different forms. The examples he there cites are not exactly the same as those he had mentioned some pages earlier, but the differences are minimal. His second list names moral, esthetic, intellectual, religious, personal, and political experience. Other forms conceivably could be added to that list (e.g., educational). Dewey's six or seven examples should suffice, however, to substantiate his point that experience is readily subdivided by form, which partially at least answers the question of where the philosopher who chooses to stay with ordinary experience is to begin.

Did Dewey follow his own advice? Did he, in other words, typically start off by choosing a form of experience to investigate? Titles of several of his major works, accompanied by the implied form of experience they address, suggest he did. Books that do so include *Ethics* (moral, LW7), *Art as Experience* (esthetic, LW10), *A Common Faith* (religious, LW9), *The Public and Its Problems* (political, LW2), *Human Nature and Conduct* (personal, MW14), and *Democracy and Education* (educational, MW9).

What of *Experience and Nature*? What form of experience does *it* address? Dewey might have called it "intellectual," though, as suggested above, I prefer to call it "philosophical." For the book as a whole, as I read it, addresses philosophical experience as pursued over the centuries. It remarks on how philosophy emerged historically and how it has changed over time. Yet its perspective is more than historical. Dewey is also sharply critical of philosophy's past and does not hesitate to call attention to its shortcomings. But the book also contains more than criticism. It makes a positive contribution as well as a negative one.

Viewed positively, it offers its readers a treatise on how philosophy ought to be pursued today, or at least how Dewey thought it should have been pursued in his time. In fact, it starts with an exploration of that question, as we have already seen. Moreover, the book as a whole goes far beyond the fragmentary suggestions about how to proceed contained in its first chapter. Beginning with Chapter 2 Dewey launches upon an actual demonstration of his own philosophic method. He *enacts* it, one might say, on almost every page. He practices throughout what he has preached in the book's first chapter.

Let us now return to the question of what goes on in the philosopher's professional practice once the choice of a form of experience has been made. At the start of Chapter 1 Dewey provides a very abbreviated answer to that question: "We may begin with experience in gross, experience in its primary and crude forms . . . and by means of its distinguishing features and its distinctive trends, note something of the constitution of the world which generates and maintains it" (LW1, 366).

Those few words harbor a vast amount of information about what Dewey believes philosophers are to do once they have chosen a form of experience to investigate. It takes a bit of unpacking, however, to bring that information to light.

The phrase "distinguishing features and distinctive trends" tells us two things about these crude forms of experience. It says that they can be further brought into focus by attending to their distinguishing features, which presumably are relatively stable. It also says that they exhibit distinctive trends, which means that they change over time. The philosopher's task, at least in part, is to identify those enduring yet changing characteristics and in so doing to "note something of the constitution of the world which generates and maintains" that special form of experience. I take that latter requirement to mean that the philosopher is obliged to say something about the function or functions served by that form of experience, something about its place in the worldly scheme of things.

How do philosophers characteristically go about those tasks? They do so by backing away from the nitty gritty, by distancing themselves from the details of immediate situations. They ascend by whatever means necessary to the heights of abstraction. They seek a bird's-eye view of things. Not to be confused, incidentally, with a "God's-eye view" of things, which would mean a view from *beyond* experience. The latter is precisely what Dewey believes philosophy incapable of delivering. Such a view, quite simply, is inconceivable.

It is here, I believe, that Dewey's recourse to the metaphor of mapmaking begins to make sense. The philosopher *is* like a mapmaker, surveying the situation from afar. Her task is to provide direction to those immersed in the details of whatever form of experience lies within the purview of her scrutiny.

Here is Dewey introducing the mapmaking metaphor near the close of the chapter we have been discussing:

> The empirical method points out when and where and how things of a designated description have been arrived at. It places before others *a map of the road that has been travelled*; they may accordingly, if they will, *re-travel the road* to *inspect the landscape* for themselves (LW1, 389, emphasis added).

A few pages later he returns to the same figure of speech, this time more subtly expressed:

> An empirical finding is refuted not by denial that one finds things to be thus and so, but by giving *directions for a course of experience* that results in finding its opposite to be the case. To convince of error as well as to lead to truth is to assist another *to see and find something which he hitherto has failed to find and recognize.* All of the wit and subtlety of reflection and of dialectic find scope in *the elaboration and conveying of directions that intelligibly point out a course to be followed* (LW1, 391, emphasis added).

But the philosopher's task, even though performed at a high level of abstraction, involves far more than description. It is also theoretical in outlook and therefore imaginatively productive. Its "issue," as Dewey said at the start, is no less than a theory of nature, the world, the universe. As he later will make clear, it must also be critical, evaluative, and judgmental. It must perform in all of those different ways if it is to fulfill its function as a humane undertaking.

AN INTERIM SUMMARY

Having arrived at this tentative if somewhat grandiose portrayal of philosophy's task, let us pause to look back at the terrain already traveled. Loosely rephrased, what our analysis of Dewey's chapter has yielded so far can be summarized in three sets of statements, each falling under a main point. They are as follows:

1. *To the committed empiricist the term experience is all-inclusive.* Its dominion is absolute. All objects, events, and imaginings are experienced occurrences. All hypothesized and idealized states of affairs, which are themselves portions of experience, are essentially proposals for action awaiting future empirical testing.
2. *Philosophy's province covers all of experience.* Its subject matter is therefore unlimited. It may commence its explorations either with the refined forms of experience that comprise the sciences or with the ordinary forms of experience that comprise the affairs of everyday life. It is with reference to the latter, however, that all of its explorations are expected to be of consequence in the long run.
3. *Philosophy's task, figuratively speaking, calls for looking upon the various forms of experience from afar.* This means surveying them from a perspective sufficiently far removed from the details of daily life to allow the distinctive characteristics of each form to show forth. The philosopher then reflects upon the worldly conditions that likely generate and sustain that form of experience. Philosophy's aim in the long run is to criticize present practices and customs, thereby seeking to contribute to their improvement.

PHILOSOPHY'S METHOD: DENOTATION

With the above summary as background, I now want to turn to something that Dewey says in relation to the contents of the second of those three summary paragraphs. Having pointed out that the philosopher is free to initiate his or her investigation almost anywhere within the limitless domain of experience, and having dealt with the objection that this lack of limits threatens to leave the philosopher at sea (it doesn't really, we discover, because there turn out to be a relatively small number of *forms* of experience to choose from), Dewey goes on to point out that the objection is actually welcome. Why so? Because it helps to uncover "the exact meaning of a truly empirical method." It does so, we learn,

> for it reveals the fact that experience for philosophy is method, not distinctive subject-matter. And it also reveals the sort of method that philosophy needs (LW1, 371).

Experience for philosophy is method, not distinctive subject matter. The dependent clause in that sentence repeats what has already been said, which is that philosophers may begin anywhere, philosophy has no distinctive subject matter. But what of the independent clause? What does it mean to say that "experience for philosophy is method"? The question turns out to be more important than it might appear, for Dewey uses the phrase repeatedly throughout the remainder of the chapter, sometimes shortening it to "experience is method." And what does he mean when he goes on to suggest that philosophy's *lack* of a distinctive subject matter reveals the *kind* of method it requires? What kind of method can that be?

Dewey is not long in providing at least partial answers to those questions. He begins with, "The value of experience as method in philosophy is that it compels us to note that *denotation* comes first and last" (LW1, 371). He follows with a series of statements that go on to explain what the process of denotation entails. It requires, he says, "that to settle any discussion, to still any doubt, to answer any question, we must go to some thing pointed to, denoted, and find our answer in that thing" (LW1, 372). A bit further on he speaks of

> the finality and comprehensiveness of the method of pointing, finding, showing, and the necessity of seeing what is pointed to and accepting what is found in good faith and without discount (LW1, 372).

To this he adds, "we need the notion of experience to remind us that 'reality' includes whatever is denotatively found" (LW1, 372).

Denotation's Difficulties

The prominence that Dewey gives to the notion of denotation did not succeed, at least not initially, in putting to rest for me the questions I earlier raised with respect to the rather enigmatic formulation "experience is method." If anything, it only increased their urgency. "What is going on here?" I wanted to know. "Why all this attention to pointing and showing," activities that on the face of it seem so closely linked to visually observable objects and to the work of physical scientists? Is there more to denotation than meets the eye? And even if it is not limited to physical objects, why call denotation a "method"? What other "method" could there be? And what does Dewey mean by the "finality" of such a method and the necessity of accepting its outcomes in "good faith"? Does not such language carry the flavor of doctrines that Dewey abhors?

I am not sure that I can answer all of those questions satisfactorily. I further doubt that Dewey could have done so in 1925. In fact, I feel reasonably certain that he could not have, for he later plays down the idea of denotation considerably, as we will subsequently see. I have come to understand, however, or think I have, why he introduced the notion in the first place and why he gave it such an essential role in his depiction of philosophy's task.

His goal in this chapter, we recall, is to explore the relation between experience and philosophic method. His basic conviction, as we have seen, is that experience is absolute. Its objects and events constitute reality. Reality includes physical objects and events, but it is by no means limited to them. It also includes, he says, all things "done, suffered, and imagined." Those objects and events that constitute reality themselves become known (realized) through the process that Dewey is here calling denotation. In short, denotation is our only way of attending to portions of experience, of picking those portions out. It is also a form of social exchange, a way of indicating to oneself and to others what one means and of calling attention to what objects mean. It is, furthermore, a crucial step in the process of adding to and enlarging upon meaning.

How does one denote? One denotes, Dewey says, by "pointing, finding, showing." These are all ways of doing something. One denotes by acting on one's environment, by altering it in certain ways, by selecting and rejecting portions of it, by making distinctions within it.

All of those ways of engaging with the world of experience comprise the method of denotation.

But why refer to denotation as philosophy's *method*? What is methodical about it? And with what other method or methods might it be compared? What are the alternatives?

Dewey did have an alternative philosophical method in mind. He called it "rationalism." It was the way of those philosophers who in their work relied chiefly if not exclusively on "logical derivation from rational ideas." The philosophers he had in mind historically were of two sorts. On the one side were the transcendentalists, whose reasoning led them to escape the world of experience and dwell in the objectless world of absolute idealism. On the other were the sensualists, whose reasoning also led them to abandon the world of ordinary objects and events and to enter a world of sensa and qualia in search of the atomic building blocks of human knowledge. Oddly enough, these two forms of rationalism were archenemies. Both were still obliged, however, to employ empirical subject matter in their arguments. They therefore made use of denotation in at least a minimal way. As Dewey pointed out, "there is nothing else for them to go by" (LW1, 391). But they did not employ the so-called method wholeheartedly. They did not acknowledge it to be their *way*, as did Dewey. It is for this reason that he considered them to be nonempirical.

Is Dewey's advocacy of denotation a surreptitious form of absolutism, an absolute realism in disguise? Not at all. Neither pointing nor showing yields the truth transparently. Denotation's apparent finality does not still doubt forever. It only provides the grounds of "good faith." It justifies belief and firms up one's convictions, true enough, but does so only temporarily. The objects of denotation are always open to change. What appears to be true can always be overturned. As the light changes (in figurative terms), so do one's beliefs.

Denotation as a Plea for Engagement in Human Affairs

Returning to the question of whether denotation is properly looked upon as a method, I must say that I fail to see it as deserving that designation, even though I have a suspicion about why Dewey may have found the term *method* attractive. I think its kinship with the term *scientific method* may have been one major source of its attraction. More on that later.

In any case, it seems clear that Dewey did not look upon the *method* of denotation as being at all methodical in the usual sense of the word.

He certainly did not see it as entailing a step-by-step procedure, for example. This becomes progressively clearer as we follow his use of the term through the remainder of the chapter. As one reads on it becomes increasingly evident that Dewey's talk about "experience as method" and his call for philosophers to make use of the method of denotation was basically an impassioned plea for them to become wholeheartedly engaged in the full range and total complexity of human affairs.[7] It was, as Dewey himself puts it, a "plea to take the conception of experience with the utmost naïveté and catholicity" (LW1, 370), "a call to open the eyes and the ears of the mind" (LW1, 373). It was also, he said, "a doctrine of humility" (LW1, 373).

The two closing sentences of the chapter sound the moral of Dewey's message with special force.

> Intellectual piety toward experience is a pre-condition of the direction of life and of tolerant and generous cooperation among men. Respect for the things of experience alone brings with it such a respect for others, the centres of experience, as is free from patronage, domination and the will to impose (LW1, 392).

The polemical nature of Dewey's call for philosophy's full engagement with human affairs deserves a few additional comments before we move on. His posture toward the two views that he explicitly opposes—he refers to those who hold them as the "transcendentalists" and the "sensualists"—is far more dismissive than argumentative. He does not seek to answer his opponents so much as to turn his back on them. "A problem of knowledge in general," which has been the source of countless philosophic treatises over the centuries, is, he says, "to speak brutally, nonsense." He twice calls the sensualist position "absurd." He repeatedly warns and cautions his readers against falling for such "simple" notions. But he never quite makes clear why such absurd ideas were so attractive in the first place and why they have remained so for so many prominent "thinkers" over so many years. Why, indeed, have so many philosophers drifted so far away from the everyday sense of experience? What exactly are the flaws of reasoning that have led them astray? Dewey does indeed offer crude answers to those questions in the material we have been examining, and it is doubtlessly unfair to expect more than that within the confines of a single chapter and an introductory one at that. Yet a sense that a great deal more could be said, both pro and con, with respect to a number of the views that Dewey summarily dismisses must surely have troubled many of his more exacting listeners and readers back in 1925.

Today, thanks to the writings of Wittgenstein, Quine, Sellars, Putnam, Davidson, McDowell, and many others, we are far better equipped than earlier readers to see what some of the flaws were in at least some of the views that Dewey so readily rejected. What has emerged, especially in the years following Dewey's death, is a sustained and penetrating critique of the empirical tradition, one that has revealed several of the tradition's latent "dogmas," as Quine (1980) has so famously dubbed them, and has resulted in what might be called empiricism's pragmatic turn. What now seems increasingly apparent is that many who over the years called themselves empiricists clung to the hope of establishing a nonempirical basis for their empiricism. They sought to transcend experience by positing an atomic particle of knowledge that was not itself learned or acquired. Could these be close relatives of the "many thinkers" that Dewey complained about in the opening paragraphs of his introductory chapter—those who endorsed empiricism but retained a deep distrust of the "subjective" dimension of experience? Perhaps not, but they sound suspiciously alike.

I am not trying to suggest here that Dewey was far ahead of his time and that he actually anticipated the arguments that Quine gives, for example, in his "Two Dogmas of Empiricism" (1980, 20–46) or those that Sellars lays out so painstakingly in his critique of "The Myth of the Given" (1997). But I do believe that in retrospect it is possible and even helpful to view both sets of critical endeavors—Dewey's and those of the more contemporary critics—as moving toward each other on convergent trajectories. I will have more to say about this possibility in succeeding chapters.

DEWEY'S DISCOMFORT WITH THE ORIGINAL VERSION OF CHAPTER 1

As I pointed out in the Introduction, in his Preface to the revised second edition of *Experience and Nature* (1929) Dewey had some harsh things to say about the version of Chapter 1 that we have just finished examining. He called it "rather confused in mode of presentation, and at one important point in thought as well" (LW1, 3). He also saw it as being "upon the whole more technical and harder reading than the chapters which it was supposed to introduce" (LW1, 3). He set out to correct those faults in the revision that we will look at next. In order to judge how successful he was in making those corrections it would be good to know something more about the nature of the defects as he saw them. Independent of whatever judgments we might come to on our own about such matters, what exactly did Dewey or other of his readers see as confusing or difficult about the original presentation? Though lacking a definitive answer to that question, we do have at least a piece of the answer in the form of an exchange of letters between Dewey and one of his friendliest critics.

Max Otto's Letter to Dewey

In December of 1928, some three years after *Experience and Nature* was published, Dewey heard from Max Otto, a professor of philosophy at the University of Wisconsin. In his letter Otto spoke of what troubled him in his reading of the book. Specifically, he complained that

> You make a distinction between method and content and insist upon phi-losophy as method. But . . . if one takes you seriously as to method, he will have a content which he would not have if he chose the rationalistic method.

Otto's letter continues, without break,

> It seems to me that there is no way to avoid the use of experience as mean-ing different things, not only for different people, but for the same people. Little more can be done, I think than to indicate this fact and to keep the different meanings distinct (LW1, 408).

He then repeats his initial complaint, again without break.

> Moreover, I am persuaded that the adoption of a certain method implies certain things as found and certain things as not found. I mean that there is no philosophic method which even as method leaves its user neutral as to the content of experience (LW1, 408).

I have purposely inserted breaks in the letter's continuous para-graph because it seems to me that the observation contained in its middle passage is somewhat tangential to the single point being made in the passages coming before and after. I take that single point to be that there can be no universal method, that is, one that fits all subject matters, as Dewey implies in the formula "experience for philosophy is method, not distinctive subject-matter."

Dewey does not comment on Otto's point that experience means different things for different people and even sometimes for the same person. Otto believes that all we can do is to note such differences and move on. Would Dewey agree? On the basis of what we have seen him say in the original first chapter, I think the answer has to be yes and no. He would have no difficulty acknowledging that the term *experience* covers both the world of experienced objects and the process of experiencing. Sometimes, in normal discourse, the term is restricted to one of those designated references and sometimes to the other. Dewey would have no unease about that kind of differential meaning. Where he would draw the line with respect to such a relaxed attitude, it seems to me, is in allowing the term to be restricted to only a portion of its normal applications. Otto's brief comment does not make clear how far his own live-and-let-live attitude would extend. In short, Dewey's universalized extension of the conception of experience, which I have already described as "absolute empiricism," is not, for him, simply one choice among many. It defines the logical space within which choice operates. Philosophy has no choice but to operate within that space as well.

Dewey's Reply to Otto

Dewey replied to Otto a month later, saying,

> I can't tell you how illuminating was your passage in which you quoted my sentence about exp. as method not subject-matter. It is ridiculous how that one thing opened up to me what was wrong in the chapter. I mean it is now ridiculous that I shouldn't have seen it before. What I meant—only didn't know it—was that *reflective analysis* & its products form a *method* for leading back to the *subject-matter* of direct or "gross" experience; so that the *former* designates or denotes a path & projects a goal to be found in the latter—which being illuminated, clarified & directed by reflective findings as method, *also* tests and checks the latter. I don't know whether I have succeeded in stating it, but my own mind has cleared up enormously (LW1, 408, emphasis in original).

Dewey still doesn't say exactly what was wrong in the chapter or why Otto's observation was so illuminating, but what we begin to see in his response to Otto is the emergence of a far more differentiated conception of the idea of method, one that presumably will replace the simplified version presented in the original first chapter. That greater differentiation is especially evident in the multiplicity of verb forms contained in Dewey's description. There are eleven such forms in all. They include "form," "leading back," "designates," "denotes," "projects," "found," "illuminated," "clarified," "directed," "tests," and "checks." It is significant that "denotes" is only one of those many forms. Additionally, there are the new key terms of "reflective analysis and its products," "path," and "goal" added to the familiar "method," "subject-matter," and "direct or 'gross' experience." The process as a whole is also far more contextualized. It is depicted as something going on within a particular location rather than something whose subject was "a theory of nature, the world, the universe." In sum, that greater differentiation of method gives us something to look for in our examination of the revised first chapter.

Dewey's repeated use of the word *ridiculous* in referring to his own failure to catch the shortcomings that Otto's letter brought to his attention expresses the way most of us would feel under similar circumstances, I presume. Its spontaneous character also reminds us of how very common it is to undergo such experiences. Indeed, it may prompt us to wonder about their inevitability. Can one completely escape feeling ridiculous when confronted with something one has overlooked? And can one ever completely avoid overlooking something? Such questions surface almost naturally as we proceed to examine Dewey's successive attempts to introduce *Experience and Nature*.

CHAPTER 2

The 1929 Preface and Revised Version of Chapter 1

One of the most endearing features of John Dewey's personality was his openness to ideas and suggestions whatever their source. At the very height of his philosophical career and even toward its very close, he was always sensitive to the possibility of new facets and dimensions of experience, to new problems and to new aspects of old problems. He was rarely satisfied with his own formulations. What he sent to the press was never a final version of his ideas but the latest draft of a position which was not yet completely thought out in his own mind and which he sincerely hoped would be developed by others.

—Sidney Hook in Morgenbesser, *Dewey and His Critics,* 1977, 9

What is the aim of philosophy? To respond to the particular question asked, and to get satisfying answers. And satisfaction is not had, and philosophy is not done, once and for all.

—Stanley Cavell, *Themes Out of School,* 1984, 234

In 1929, in preparation for his book's fourth printing, Dewey added a Preface and substituted a new first chapter to replace the one that had originally served as introduction to *Experience and Nature.* He did so, as has been explained, to overcome weaknesses that he had belatedly discovered in the book's original first chapter. The newly added Preface and the newly written first chapter were designed to repair those faults. Our interest in both documents is essentially comparative. We are chiefly concerned with how the new and revised material adds to or modifies the conception of the relationship between experience and philosophic method presented in the original first chapter.

THE PREFACE

Before presenting a chapter-by-chapter overview of his book's contents, which is the main purpose of the Preface, Dewey offers a summary of what he calls "the thought of the book in the order of its development," which is his way of saying what the book as a whole is all about. His desire in writing *Experience and Nature*, he begins, was

> to apply in the more general realm of philosophy the thought which is effective in dealing with any and every genuine question, from the elaborate problems of science to the practical deliberations of daily life, trivial or momentous (LW1, 3).

I take the meaning of that sentence as straightforward, though it does contain a couple of words and one longer expression that seem to me worthy of comment.

Dewey says, in essence, that his book's orientation will be methodological. His goal is to apply in the general realm of philosophy the same way of thinking that works so well elsewhere in dealing with questions. He adds the qualifier "genuine" to "questions," which alerts us to the possibility of questions that are *not* genuine. Though he does not say so, the veiled implication is that philosophy may be peculiarly vulnerable to nongenuine questions.

His expression "in the general realm of philosophy" can only puzzle those of us who have just finished examining his original first chapter. For there, one of his major points was that philosophy does not have any distinctive subject matter. He portrayed it as free to traverse all of experience.

What might Dewey mean, then, in speaking of philosophy's *realm*? The interpretation I give the word might not be the same as Dewey's, but it is at least consistent with what he says about philosophy in the original first chapter. I imagine "the more general realm of philosophy," as he puts it, to be *the realm of the more general*, which is to say, the more general in whatever domain of experience (on whichever of its "forms") the philosopher happens to be working. My way of putting it explicitly acknowledges the high level of abstraction at which philosophers typically operate. This feature of their way of working, which was briefly mentioned in the last chapter, will be referred to increasingly as we move along.

Dewey's use of the word *thought* to describe what it is that gets applied in his conception of philosophy underscores the intellectual nature of the activity. His mention of *questions* and *problems* makes clear its instrumental value.

Having established the applied intellectual focus of philosophy, Dewey moves on to say something about "the constant task" of all such effective thought. It is "to establish working connections between old and new subject-matters." Notice the way Dewey's exposition at this point instantiates the very method whose operation he is describing. Though just beginning to talk about philosophy, he has already ascended to the realm of *the more general*.

Remaining at that high level of abstraction, he next describes the form in which the inevitable confrontation between "old and new subject-matters" becomes most urgently manifest in today's world. Currently, he says,

> modern science, modern industry, and politics have presented us with an immense amount of material foreign to, often inconsistent with, the most prized intellectual and moral heritage of the modern world (LW1, 4).

That set of conditions, Dewey tells us, "sets the especial problem for philosophy today and for many days to come" (LW1, 4).

Philosophy's task is not to attempt a superficial reconciliation of the old and the new. Rather, it is to employ "a body of old beliefs and ideas to apprehend and understand the new," while keeping in mind "the modifications and transformations that are exacted of those old beliefs" (LW1, 4).

In the light of those circumstances and in response to that urgent need, Dewey proceeds to voice his own conviction and with it his book's plan.

> I believe that the method of empirical naturalism presented in this volume provides the way, and the only way—although no two thinkers will travel it in the same way—by which one can freely accept the standpoint and conclusions of modern science: the way by which we can be genuinely naturalistic and yet maintain cherished values, provided they are critically clarified and reinforced (LW1, 4).

Commentary

What I find particularly striking about that statement—apart from its containing the initial appearance of the term *empirical naturalism*, a term that will occupy our attention more fully in due course—is the odd way it boldly asserts, then quickly blunts the force of its assertions, rather like a boxer who pulls his punches. Empirical naturalism is said to be "the only way," yet in a twinkling we learn that "no two thinkers will travel it in the same way." How can the *only* way leave room for such differences, one wonders?

We next are told that we can have the standpoint and conclusions of science *plus* our cherished values, *provided* the latter are "critically clarified and reinforced." Another straightforward assertion gets partially withdrawn by the words that immediately follow it. One imagines some readers might think, "But what if a part of what one cherishes about those values is precisely their avowed permanence? What if one does not *want* to have them critically clarified and reinforced? Has one then left the path of empirical naturalism completely or is one still traveling it, but in a different way?" I do not introduce such a hypothetical questioner in order to mock Dewey. Nor am I suggesting that his statement contains blatant contradictions. It clearly does not. Yet it does seem to harbor some internal tensions that call for resolution. Those same tensions or ones closely related to them will reemerge more than once as we proceed.

Dewey goes on to assure his readers that the "main purport" of empirical naturalism is not to be destructive. Rather it is to operate like "a winnowing fan," getting rid of "the chaff." While not exactly trying to "save" anything, it nonetheless inspires "the mind with courage and vitality to create new ideals and values in the face of the perplexities of a new world" (LW1, 4).[1]

Though clearly intended to allay concern on the part of those inclined to be fearful of change, the winnowing fan imagery is hardly the most comforting anodyne that Dewey might have chosen. The task at hand, however, has less to do with the aptness of Dewey's figures of speech than with trying to figure out what they may tell us about his conception of the philosopher's task. The image of the winnowing fan does communicate something crucial about that task. It reveals philosophy to be a critical endeavor. The philosopher may not set out to destroy cherished values, true enough, but her candid investigation of recurring forms of experience cannot avoid being judgmental. Such judgments are almost bound to be threatening to some, Dewey's reassurances to the contrary notwithstanding.

An additional fragment of figurative language in Dewey's opening statement begs our attention. It is his use of the word *travel*, as in "no two thinkers will travel it in the same way." He introduces the term when referring to the variability that remains once the method of empirical naturalism has been adopted.

As has been said, Dewey often draws upon travel imagery when trying to describe the philosopher at work. In the last chapter we noted his use of the metaphor of the philosopher as mapmaker. We have more to say about that metaphor later on in this chapter. We also treat the topic of figurative language and its place in describing philosophy's task at some length in Chapter 4. For now we need only note that despite its sounding a bit odd, there is nothing intrinsically contradictory about the notion that philosophers have but one way to go (the way of empirical naturalism) yet many ways of getting there. Many are the paths that lead to Rome.

Dewey next turns to the contents of the new introductory chapter. He says only a bit about it in just a single paragraph.

> The new introductory chapter (Chapter 1) accordingly takes up the question of method, especially with respect to the relation that exists between experience and nature. It points to faith in experience when intelligently used as a means of disclosing the realities of nature. It finds that nature and experience are not enemies or alien. Experience is not a veil that shuts man off from nature; it is a means of penetrating continually further into the heart of nature. There is in the character of human experience no index-hand pointing to agnostic conclusions, but rather a growing progressive self-disclosure of nature itself. The failures of philosophy have come from lack of confidence in the directive powers that inhere in experience, if men had but the wit and courage to follow them (LW1, 4–5).

The two most noteworthy phrases in that paragraph are "faith in experience when intelligently used" and "the directive powers that inhere in experience." Of those two, the latter probably contains more methodological implications than the former, although the two are not easily distinguishable in those terms. Their joint message is that faith in experience is actually faith in the power of experience to direct our next move in life (and all subsequent moves as well), provided, of course, that we have the courage and the wit (i.e., the intelligence) to follow its directives. Moreover, the roots of that faith presumably inhere in experience itself. It is therefore a direct outgrowth of experience, a faith both *in* and *of* experience.

But the faith in and of experience that is said to be characteristic of empirically minded philosophers and that Dewey promises to take up in Chapter 1, the doctrine he refers to as "empirical naturalism," must in some way be different from the faith in experience of the physical scientist, let us say, or that of the average person facing life's daily problems. Were that not so, were there nothing distinctive about empirical naturalism as a specifically *philosophical* doctrine, Dewey seemingly would have nothing further to say. The admonition for philosophers to be empirical would then reduce to telling them simply to behave like scientists, in the one instance, or to follow the dictates of common sense, in the other.

To see what he does have to say on the subject, let us now turn to the revised chapter.

THE NEW INTRODUCTORY CHAPTER

Dewey points out at the start of his Preface that the new first chapter was entirely rewritten. This makes a line-by-line or even a paragraph-by-paragraph comparison of the old and the new versions virtually impossible. The two have few if any sentences in common, much less whole paragraphs or pages. Since the two versions are roughly equal in length, one very crude way of comparing them is by looking at the relative frequencies of several key words or phrases in both chapters. I have made that comparison, using thirteen such words or phrases, with the results shown in Table 2.1.

As that table reveals, the four words or terms that newly appear in the revised version are *ordinary experience, primary experience, reflective analysis,* and *reflective.* There is also in the revised version a marked decline in the frequencies of *denote, denotative method,* and *science,* along with a noticeable increase in the use of *empirical method, philosophy,* and *nature.* What those differences mean is far from clear, but are at least suggestive of a shift in the direction of an increased differentiation between philosophy's method and that of the sciences. With that as a kind of working hypothesis, let us turn to the text itself.

The chapter opens with this one-sentence paragraph:

> The title of this volume, Experience and Nature, is intended to signify that the philosophy here presented may be termed either empirical naturalism or naturalistic empiricism, or, taking "experience" in its usual signification, naturalistic humanism (LW1, 10).

Table 2.1. Frequency of Key Words and Phrases in Original and
Revised Versions of Chapter 1.

Word or Phrase	Original Version	Revised Version
Experience	142	209
Ordinary (ordinary experience)	0	16
Primary experience	0	23
Nature	17	54
Philosophy	27	50
Empirical method	18	33
Science	24	14
Denote	16	5
Denotation (denotative method)	12	2
Reflective analysis	0	4
Reflective	0	18
Reflection	19	28

The sentence is puzzling in the choice it offers. Even more puzzling is the suggestion that the choice of the three terms is somehow implicit in the book's title. How are readers to have known that? Or is Dewey not suggesting that they should? And what are readers to make of those three terms? What is meant by *empirical naturalism*? Or *naturalistic empiricism*? Or *naturalistic humanism*?

Almost in answer to that spate of questions Dewey goes on to say,

> To many the associating of the two words [experience and nature] will seem like talking of a round square, so engrained is the notion of the separation of man and experience from nature (LW1, 10).

Notice, however, what two words Dewey is talking about. He is not referring to any of the pairs of words that appear in his opening sentence. He is talking about how some people may respond to the title of his book.

Who might they be, these readers for whom the separation of *experience* and *nature* is so deeply engrained that they cannot even begin to deal with having the two terms placed side by side in the book's title? Dewey has three candidates for those supposedly suffering from such closed-mindedness. First, there are those who acknowledge experience to be important but of little use in revealing "the nature of Nature." It is hard to guess who these might be, but I presume he means absolute realists, those who believe in a reality (Nature) that can never be known. Next come those who look upon experience as actually concealing nature, as forming a kind of veil or screen that must somehow be penetrated or brushed aside if we are to confront reality directly. These presumably are those sometimes referred to as materialistic realists. They believe that all of experience is ultimately translatable into physicalistic terms. Finally, there are those of "an opposite school," as Dewey says, who favor experience over nature and who propose arriving at transcendent truth by turning their backs on nature entirely. These, we guess, are philosophy's absolute idealists.

How does Dewey propose dealing with such misguided individuals? His answer is illuminating not only for what it says about his own conception of philosophy's method but also for the light it sheds on the puzzle with which my own investigation began—the question of why Dewey seemed to be having difficulty in introducing *Experience and Nature*.

Here is what he says about the problem of converting to his own way of thinking the three kinds of disbelievers that he has named.

> I know of no route by which dialectical argument can answer such objections. They arise from associations with words and cannot be dealt with argumentatively. One can only hope in the course of the whole discussion to disclose the meanings which are attached to "experience" and "nature," and thus insensibly produce, if one is fortunate, a change in the significations previously attached to them (LW1, 10).

By "the course of the whole discussion" Dewey presumably means the entirety of the book he is in the process of introducing. But he could as easily be referring to his life's work as a whole, for the issue and his attempt to deal with it extend far beyond the contents of *Experience and Nature*. They constitute the central theme of almost all of his writings.

His strategy in dealing with the problem, both here and elsewhere, is not to resort to close argument. Nor does he engage in one-on-one intellectual combat. To do so would bring him too close to the strategy of the rationalists, with whom he disagrees and from whom he wishes to remain apart.[2]

Instead he adopts a much looser and more meandering form of argument. He circles his topic, approaching it now from this angle and now from that. He introduces a line of reasoning and then drops it, only to pick it up again a bit further on. That strategy, incidentally, helps to account for one of the qualities that Dewey's readers often complain about: the repetitiveness evident in his writing.

One of his favorite rhetorical devices is to draw an analogy between the activities of science and the work of philosophy. In science, Dewey points out, "nature and experience get along harmoniously together" (LW1,11). The hope is that they someday will do so in philosophy as well. He warns that the comparison with science is not supposed to prove anything with respect to the worth of empirical naturalism for philosophical doctrine. It should, however, at least "weaken those verbal associations which stand in the way of apprehending the force of empirical method in philosophy" (LW1, 13).

The chief reason that experience and nature get along so harmoniously in science is that the scientific investigator "assumes as a matter of course that experience, controlled in specifiable ways, is the avenue that leads to the facts and laws of nature" (LW1, 11). The scientist, in other words, has "faith" in experience, a faith that philosophers, by and large, do not have.

There are other, more concrete comparisons between philosophy and science that Dewey continually reiterates. Among them are the following:

The beginning and ending of investigation. The scientist, Dewey tells us, always starts with ordinary experience and invariably returns there. She may use very sophisticated instruments and very refined forms of reasoning, but the scientist's "pendant of theory," as Dewey refers to it in one passage, "is attached at both ends to the pillars of observed subject-matter." Those scientific practices reveal what Dewey calls "the primacy and ultimacy of ordinary experience" (LW1, 24).

The theories of present-day philosophy, by way of contrast, are usually unattached at both ends. They respect neither the primacy nor the ultimacy of ordinary experience. They begin with the products of refined thought (often borrowed from science), and they seldom bother to test their own refinements on that thought by returning them to the tribunal of ordinary experience, as scientists (in Dewey's view) routinely do.

The implications of such a comparison are obvious. Philosophers are urged by Dewey to behave more like scientists. They should start off with what he calls "genuine" problems, which is to say, problems evinced in ordinary experience, and they should return to those problems upon completion of their own excursions into the realm of refined and systematic thought.

The necessity of sustained, systematic thought. Though science may begin and end in ordinary experience, it obviously requires sustained, systematic thought. This usually means being divorced for at least a time from the necessity of taking action and of being involved in worldly affairs. Dewey's way of acknowledging that requirement is to speak of science as primarily a form of intellectual experience.

Philosophy too is an intellectual endeavor, clearly enough. Its practitioners also must for a time remain engrossed in thought. The trouble with too many philosophers, Dewey believes, is that they stay there forever, never returning to the world of ordinary affairs.

There is another consequence of remaining too long in the realm of abstraction. It is that intellectual or cognitive experience begins to take on a degree of importance that elevates it above all other forms of experiencing. Dewey calls this *intellectualism*.

The necessity of systematic exclusion. Science is always selectively attentive. It looks at some things and ignores others. It must do so in order to advance. Its only obligation with respect to such a necessity is to acknowledge the choices being made, the reasons for making them, and the procedures for carrying them out. It is furthermore obliged at some later stage to demonstrate the benefits that accrue from having made those choices.

Philosophers too must attend to some things and ignore others. In acting on that necessity, however, philosophers, according to Dewey, too often fail to acknowledge the choices that have been made. They also do not make public the grounds for these choices. In some cases they do something even worse, Dewey complains. They take the object of their reflection, which is usually the product of refined thought, and proceed to hypostatize or even sanctify it. They ascribe to it, in other words, an elevated status within the domain of reality that other, more commonplace objects do not enjoy. Here is how he puts it.

> Now the standing temptation of philosophy, as its course abundantly demonstrates, is to regard the results of reflection as having, in and of themselves, a reality superior to that of the material of any other mode of experience.

> The commonest assumption of philosophies, common even to philosophies very different from one another, is the assumption of the identity of objects of knowledge and ultimately real objects. The assumption is so deep that it is usually not expressed; it is taken for granted as something so fundamental that it does not need to be stated (LW1, 27).

Dewey refers to this maneuver as one form of "*the* philosophical fallacy" (LW1, 51).

The need to convince others. Science is a communal affair. Its progress and vitality depend on scientists' coming to accept each other's conclusions and making use of them in their own work. That degree of acceptance requires being able to replicate the findings of others. Dewey describes the procedure by which that occurs thusly:

> The scientific investigator convinces others not by the plausibility of his definitions and the cogency of his dialectic, but by placing before them the specified course of searchings, doings and arrivals, in consequence of which certain things have been found. His appeal is for others to traverse a similar course, so as to see how what they find corresponds with his report (LW1, 34).

What I find to be especially noteworthy about that description is the way it subtly incorporates figurative language having to do with physical travel. A more elaborate interweaving of the same figure of speech occurs in an extended passage in which Dewey explains how the scientist moves back and forth from secondary or reflective experience to primary experience. The statement is worth presenting in full because of the central question it raises with respect to philosophic method.

> But just what role do the objects attained in reflection play? Where do they come in? They explain the primary objects, they enable us to grasp them with understanding, instead of just having sense-contact with them. But how?
>   Well, they define or lay out a *path* by which return to experienced things is of such a sort that the meaning, the significant content, of what is experienced gains an enriched and expanded force because of *the path* or method by which it was reached. Directly, in immediate contact it may be just what it was before—hard, colored, odorous, etc. But when the secondary objects, the refined objects, are employed as a method or *road* for coming at them, these qualities cease to be isolated details; they get the meaning contained in a whole system of related objects; they are rendered continuous with the rest of nature and take on the import of the things they are now seen to be continuous with (LW1, 16, emphasis added).

Dewey refers to that whole procedure as "the *denotative* method" (LW1, 16). The obvious question his description raises is whether there is an analog of that back and forth movement for philosophers. Dewey seems to think there is. He says,

> The charge that is brought against the non-empirical method of philosophizing is not that it depends upon theorizing, but that it fails to use refined, secondary products as a path pointing and leading back to something in primary experience (LW1, 17).

He then proceeds to point out the consequences of that failure. They are threefold. First, there remains no way to verify philosophy's findings; second, the things of ordinary experience do not become enriched in meaning through being conjoined with the products of reflective thought; and third, philosophy's own products—those reflective thoughts themselves—remain isolated, becoming what he elsewhere calls "museum pieces."

Dewey's accusation is clear enough. The question is whether it is justified or deserved. Could philosophers move back and forth from primary to secondary experience as readily as the trope of moving along a path from one point to another makes it seem? Dewey hints that the process may be far more difficult than it might appear. Toward the end of the chapter, speaking of how one gives directions to someone for a course of experience that will lead him to find what he has hitherto failed to find and recognize, he says,

> All of the wit and subtlety of reflection and logic find scope in the elaboration and conveying of directions that intelligibly point out a course to be followed (LW1, 36).

Why might that be so? Why does it take such wit and subtlety to give such directions? That question brings us to a consideration of the limitations of the analogy between science and philosophy.

Where Does the Analogy Between Science and Philosophy Break Down?

Despite Dewey's obvious admiration for the methods of science and his clear impatience with the ways of nonempirical philosophers, he is not out to erase the distinction between the two sets of activities. Given that he would clearly like to see philosophy move in the direction of science insofar as its reliance on experience is concerned, science remains science for Dewey—and philosophy, philosophy. How does he look upon their distinctiveness and how does that bear on the question of philosophic method?

As Dewey tells the story of how modern science came into being, he presents it as an outgrowth of the perceived benefits of distinguishing between the physical and the psychological or mental and holding those two components of primary experience in temporary detachment. To make that separation, Dewey explains, is "to be set upon the road that conducts to tools and technologies, to construction of mechanisms, to the arts that ensue in the wake of the sciences" (LW1, 20).

Philosophy's subject matter is quite different from that of the sciences. It does not turn on the distinction between the physical and the psychological. Instead, it focuses on what Dewey calls "life-experience," which is a conglomeration of firsthand experience that is itself "already overlaid and saturated with the products of the reflection of past generations and by-gone ages." The union of that firsthand experience and the interpretations laid upon it by the culture of our own time and place is so intimate as to form a kind of intellectual garment that we can never totally cast off. Dewey refers to those "absorbed borrowings" as "prejudices" whose sources and authority usually remain unexamined and unacknowledged. They therefore potentially obfuscate and distort one's perception.

An empirical philosophy, says Dewey, aims at a kind of "intellectual disrobing." Though we may never be able to cast off our inherited prejudices entirely—or even want to, for that matter—we can, says Dewey, "inspect them critically to see what they are made of and what wearing them does to us" (LW1, 39). Philosophy's task, in the final analysis, is to aid in that process and thereby contribute to the "intelligent furthering of culture" (LW1, 39).

Does that description differentiate sufficiently between philosophy and science to avoid confusion? It certainly separates them figuratively. Aiding in the task of intellectual disrobing is a very different image from setting out upon the road that conducts to tools and technologies, to construction of mechanism. The distinction allows us to see philosophy as more humanistic in its scope than science, even though the latter may be commonly undertaken to serve human ends.

But what of the distinction's methodological consequences? Does it yield a clearer picture of philosophic method than the one we have managed to put together so far? I would say that it succeeds in doing so only marginally. It does bring into focus the philosopher's role as cultural critic and thereby calls attention to the task of penetrating the haze of inherited meaning that Dewey sees as engulfing all of experience. But it does so, it seems to me, at the risk of conflating the task of philosophy with that of cultural criticism in general. It forces us to ask how, if at all, the philosopher as cultural critic differs from the non-philosopher who is working the same side of the street, that is, the cultural critic plain and simple.

Also, the figurative language that Dewey introduces in what he says about cultural criticism—his point about "intellectual disrobing" and divesting oneself of the "habits" one wears—does not fit very well with what he elsewhere says about the philosopher as "map-maker," or travel guide. Pointing out "routes" and "pathways" is not the same as helping someone disrobe intellectually.

One must not make too much of such differences, naturally enough. After all, there is no law against an author's using more than one figure of speech to make his case. Nor should one be too schoolmarmish about the no-no of mixing one's metaphors. Yet the pair of figures that Dewey draws upon do seem to pull in different directions methodologically. Each has the philosopher occupied with a particular set of questions. The philosopher-as-mapmaker is keen on helping people get places. The philosopher-as-cultural-critic seems far more concerned with how to get them out of the fix they are in. This is not the place to try to resolve the tensions implicit in that difference, but it is worth noting them all the same and keeping them in mind as our exploration continues.

Before leaving this overview of Dewey's revised first chapter I want to say something additional about Dewey's attitude of impatience toward those he calls "non-empirical philosophers." There is no doubt that he finds their position annoying. He describes them as "addicted" to what is simple, "hypnotized" by the eternal (LW1, 32). He speaks of their "catalyptic rigidity" in clinging to what is dear to them (LW1, 31). He mocks their "absurd search for a philosopher's stone" (LW1, 33).

What I find intriguing is how much feeling such language communicates. As a public figure, Dewey could hardly be called passionate or emotional. His New England upbringing and taciturn manner effectively kept his private side hidden from view most of the time. Yet there can be no doubt that he did feel passionately about many of the social and political issues of his day. He also cared deeply about the role philosophy might play in addressing them.

As noted in Chapter 1, Alan Ryan (1995) has remarked on Dewey's mastery of the oratorical genre of the "lay sermon." A sermon, lay or religious, has an obvious moral purpose, as we know. It is a form of exhortation. It calls on its audience to live in a different way and in so doing it communicates a sense of caring on the part of the sermonizer. In short, it typically is infused with feeling.

A question that Dewey's occasional outbursts of impatience and scorn brings to the fore is whether one can be a philosopher *without* delivering lay sermons. More to the point, can one be a Deweyan philosopher without doing so? Is sermonizing part of such a philosopher's method? Must it be? I am not sure of the answer to that question, but I do know that there is far more to Dewey's temperament than meets the eye. The kindly sage of unruffled mien, which pictures of Dewey in his mature years so memorably depict, was not much given to barking, yet he was not without bite.

COMPARING THE REVISED CHAPTER
WITH THE ORIGINAL

We recall that in the first paragraph of the Preface to the revised edition of *Experience and Nature* Dewey acknowledged that the original first chapter had been "more technical and harder reading than the chapters which it was supposed to introduce." He expressed the hope that the revised first chapter would be found to be "both simpler and possessed of greater continuity." Do we find it so?

I confess that I do not. This is not to say that I find it to be *more* difficult than the original. I simply do not know what to say about its level of difficulty. I feel the same way with respect to the criterion of continuity.[3]

Instead of bringing me to a firm judgment about either difficulty or continuity, my reading of both versions leaves me with a very vague impression of movement in the direction of bringing empirical philosophy somewhat closer to the humanities, thereby distancing it ever so slightly from its methodological affinity with the sciences. This impression results from my noting several small differences between the two versions, some more telling than others, but each adding to the cumulative effect.

There is, first of all, the appearance of the term *naturalistic humanism* in the opening paragraph of the new chapter. That in itself is enough to signal that a shift of some kind may be under way. Even though the other two terms that Dewey offers as alternatives retain the word *empiricism*, the fact that he is willing to do without that word in one of the three choices strikes me as significant.

I next note that he also drops the suggestion that one may begin one's philosophical investigations either with the refined experience of the sciences or with ordinary experience. The former possibility is no longer presented as an alternative (not that Dewey ever seemed all that enthused about that option to begin with). I further note that the emphasis on denotation as a philosophic method has been markedly reduced. Dewey still uses the term in the revised chapter, true enough, but without the focus on finding, pointing, and showing that was in the original first chapter.

The trope of looking upon empirical philosophy as a form of intellectual disrobing is new in the revised version, as is the fuller elaboration of that figure of speech. I have already spoken of the tension between that new language and the original figure of the philosopher as mapmaker. That tension is an integral part of the shift that I am trying to describe. Also new is the expression "intelligent furthering of culture."

I have mentioned Dewey's noticeable impatience with non-empirical philosophers. Is that impatience any greater or less in the revised version than in the earlier one? I have the impression that it may be somewhat less in the new version, but I cannot say for sure. The nonempirical philosopher remains Dewey's bête noire throughout both versions and, indeed, throughout the entire book. Yet I do sense a slight reduction of the antipathy expressed in the original first chapter. Perhaps that has to do with his coming to understand that the conversion of nonempirical philosopher to an empirical point of view is not to be achieved through close dialectical argument of the kind in which philosophers have traditionally engaged. If it is to happen at all, Dewey now seems to be saying, it will occur gradually as the result of patiently explaining and reexplaining the main tenets of naturalistic humanism. As we near the end of our examination of the revised chapter, this seems as good a place as any to try to say what those main tenets now appear to be. I would summarize them thusly:

1. Commitment to an unfettered investigation of all forms of experience, both ordinary and refined.
2. Acknowledgment of the primacy and ultimacy of ordinary experience.

3. Faith in the power of intelligently examined experience to generate both the methods and criteria of improved experience.
4. Recognition of the necessity of continually moving back and forth between primary experience on the one hand and reflective thought on the other, the latter being philosophy's realm of the more general.

What this summary leaves out are any suggestions having to do with how the philosopher might decide what questions to ask or what thoughts to think during the reflective phase of her investigation. In the original chapter there appeared very fleetingly the suggestion that the most general question to ask might be: *What worldly conditions generate and sustain a form of experience such as this one?*

The closest we come to such a suggestion in the revised version is found in Dewey's talk about the philosopher as mapmaker and as cultural critic. The mapmaker implicitly tries to answer the question, Where do we go from here? The cultural critic is more intent on asking, Where have we gone wrong? How did we arrive at our present state of affairs?

The latter question is obviously related to the issue of generation and sustenence, although the one about mapmaking is not unrelated to that issue. Plainly enough, where one goes in the future is at least partially dependent on where one has been in the past. Yet the two queries do point in different directions, that much is clear, and insofar as the conduct of philosophy is concerned, each one, if pursued, would lead to a quite different philosophical orientation.

Perhaps such differences are best left unresolved at this point. It may even be that they are best left that way period. Dewey makes the point that it takes wit and subtlety to move back and forth from primary experience to reflective thought. Perhaps that is all that can be said about such matters. Yet the wish to say more persists and will continue to do so as we move on to an examination of his two incompleted manuscripts that were to serve as re-introductions to a reissue of *Experience and Nature.*

CHAPTER 3

The Two Unpublished Re-Introductions

Philosophy is surely the paradigm of that which always becomes but
never is.
                                    —*Wilfrid Sellars,* Naturalism and Ontology, *1979, viii*

Though space shines bright
And paths are trodden clear
Never to thy searching sight
Does the true road appear

Till dart th'arrows
Of thine own lifted flame
Through clinging fogs that close
And hide the journey's aim.
                                    —John Dewey, *The Poems of John Dewey,* 1977, 64–65

THE INITIAL RE-INTRODUCTION

Dewey's third attempt to introduce *Experience and Nature* was begun
in the late fall of 1948. Dewey was then eighty-nine. The occasion for
undertaking that project, as I explained in my Introduction, was the
publisher's plan to reissue the volume on or around the twenty-fifth
anniversary of its initial publication. Less than a year after he had
started on that intended re-introduction a first draft of it ran to more
than a hundred pages of typescript, double-spaced. And Dewey clearly
had more to say, when, for a variety of reasons, including a bout of
illness, he was forced to lay the work aside. He did return to the task
some two years later, but instead of picking up again where he had
left off, he began afresh.

Dewey's colleague Joseph Ratner, who edited the hundred and
more pages down to the shortened version of the manuscript that appears as an Appendix to Volume 1 of Dewey's Later Works, explains

that Dewey's original intention had been to undertake a project of "grand design—a philosophical interpretation of the history of Western man" as soon as he had finished the new introduction. For some reason, however, Dewey seems to have been unable to wait. He found himself getting caught up in that more ambitious undertaking even before finishing his work on the Re-Introduction, which is why the latter grew to such an inordinate length.

A word about Ratner's editing is in order. He reports that in preparing the manuscript for publication he was "obliged to transpose, rearrange, prune, cut up, and splice" the text, trying all the while to keep Dewey's meaning intact (LW1, 330).[1] Unfortunately, he says no more than that. Without the originl manuscript available to compare with the printed version, we are forced to take him at his word, trusting that he did indeed succeed in hewing to Dewey's original meaning. The possibility remains, of course, that he succeeded less well than he may have realized. We must keep that possibility in mind as we proceed.

Because the length of the shortened version—thirty pages or so—is roughly the same as the length of each of the two chapters we have already examined, I had initially planned to begin this chapter with a comparison of the frequencies of several key words as they appeared in all three documents. To that end I arranged the material in tabular form much like Table 2.1. I discovered, however, that the contents of Table 3.1 were not nearly as informative as I had anticipated and have therefore relegated the full table to a note.[2]

The most striking of the differences revealed by that comparison lay in the relative frequency of the word *experience*. From a high of 209 mentions in the revised (1929) version and 142 mentions in the original first chapter, it sinks to a low of 29 in the unfinished introduction. The second most striking difference was the total absence of the term *empirical method* in the unfinished introduction, a term that had appeared 18 and 33 times, respectively, in the original and revised first chapter. Among the other terms that do not show up at all in the unfinished introduction are *ordinary experience*, *primary experience*, *denote*, *denotation*, and *reflective analysis*, all of which had figured prominently in one or both of the earlier versions.

That set of differences was quite enough to convince me that whatever else the unfinished re-introduction might reveal about Dewey's conception of the philosopher's task, it could not properly be looked upon as just another attempt to repeat what was said in either of the two versions of Chapter 1. That conviction prompted me to lay such numerical comparisons aside and proceed with a more traditional examination of the text, paragraph by paragraph.

Introducing the Re-Introduction

Dewey begins by remarking on the crucially important history of the twenty-five years that have elapsed since the book was first published. That history, he says, has had a special bearing on the philosophical problem that was pointed to in his book's title—that is, the relationship between experience and nature. Our views of nature have changed dramatically, principally through the impact of science. And so have our views of human affairs, chiefly as the result of "disturbances" that

> are taking place which are sufficiently extensive and profound as to threaten what, in the hopes of some and in the fears of others, is an overturn in the entire structure of the old and supposedly firmly established order (LW1, 330).

Dewey does not pause to identify the "disturbances" he has in mind. He hardly need do so. They obviously include World War II and its aftermath, which would comprise such singular events as the rise of communism, the defeat of fascism, and the Cold War struggle between East and West.

Dewey next asks, quasi-rhetorically, how the positions he takes in his book stand up in the face of the dramatic changes of the past twenty-five years. His answer: They stand up pretty well in the main. The clearest evidence of their doing so lies in his willingness to have the text reissued without substantial change. He claims not to find "anything in the text which is seriously incompatible with what he would find it necessary to say were it written today" (LW1, 330).

The qualifier "seriously" leaves the door open, of course, to the possibility of things less than serious that he might have liked to change. But for all practical purposes, presumably, such matters can be safely overlooked.

What cannot be overlooked, however, is that the events that have taken place since the book's first publication allow Dewey's initial positions to be placed in a larger context. Dewey proposes to devote the Re-Introduction to "an exposition of that larger context" (LW1, 330).

Man and Nature: Reexamining the Relationship

When he initially wrote *Experience and Nature,* Dewey explains, the word *experience* stood for "every actual and every possible way in which man, himself a part of nature, has dealings with all other aspects and phases of nature" (LW1, 331).

Experience, in other words, stood for "the complex of all that is distinctly human" (LW1, 331). What we now can see, however, thanks to all that has happened in recent years, is

> that while "experience" is a fitting name for the special way in which man, at least in the Western world, has shaped his participations in and dealings with nature, its peculiarly distinctive application may be said to lie within the cultures that have followed from, and mark the break with, the medieval period (LW1, 331).

I take this to mean that although Dewey is not taking back anything he had earlier written having to do with the ubiquity and universality of experience, he *is* acknowledging that the concept is distinctively useful in denoting the spirit of much that has taken place within the Western world since medieval times. Indeed, the concept's very indefiniteness, which, as we may recall, Dewey had remarked upon at the start of his book's original first chapter, is one aspect of its fitness for capturing the temper of the times.

This partial curtailment of the concept's range of distinctive applicability is overcome, Dewey says,

> by the more generalized statement that the standing problem of Western philosophy throughout its entire history has been the connection-and-distinction of what on one side is regarded as human and on the other side as natural (LW1, 330).

What this means for Western philosophy is the following: Though it may have the same *standing problem* throughout its history, the *content* of that problem varies, and may even do so radically, from one historical epoch to another. The transition from medieval to modern times marks one such dramatic shift. This means, further, that philosophy cannot turn its back on those historically significant changes without divorcing itself from human affairs in general. Its continued pursuit of the eternal and the universal and its consequent splintering into "opposed doctrinal schools" has led to its current loss of esteem, Dewey contends.

This brings Dewey to a semi-definition of philosophy, which is "a highly generalized handling of human problems in connection with their setting in nature as nature is understood at a given time" (LW1, 333).

Dewey sees nothing wrong with there being variation in philosophy's proposed solutions to the problems it addresses. Heated controversy may sometimes accompany those proposals. He does note somewhat sardonically, however, that, as a rule, philosophy's central problems have more often been dissolved than solved. He concludes with the blunt observation, "What we validly know seems to indicate that process, if anything, is what is 'universal'" (LW1, 333).

Dewey next launches into a lengthy discussion of the emergence of modern scientific knowing from its Greek-medieval roots. This portion of the new introduction must surely be what Ratner was referring to when he spoke of Dewey's longterm writing plans' forcing their way into his writing of the Re-Introduction. Dewey's next job, Ratner explained, was to have been the writing of "a philosophical interpretation of the history of Western man." Something of that nature seems to be what he has launched upon in the central portion of the introduction. He begins by quoting from an address by Lord Acton, the British historian, who explains what is meant by modern history. From there he moves to a discussion of the impact of the scientific discoveries of Copernicus and Galileo upon the character and function of the concept of experience.

As interesting as it might be to trace in detail Dewey's line of thought about such matters, I am going to forego doing so for two reasons. First, because I agree with Ratner that Dewey at this juncture seems to be off on something of a tangent rather than staying with the task of re-introducing *Experience and Nature.* I suspect Dewey realized that himself when he returned to it after a two-year delay. That well may explain why he then put his previous draft aside and began afresh. Second, because of the heavy editing of the manuscript that Ratner reports having done—all of it without Dewey's knowing consent, needless to say, since it was done after he died—I feel uneasy about scrutinizing the text as though it were a finished product approved by its author. At the same time, I do want to examine it with an eye to what it might reveal about the topic that lies at the heart of the book that Dewey was re-introducing: the relationship between experience and philosophic method.

Before starting on that task I must register an objection to Ratner's depiction of the project upon which Dewey was apparently prematurely launched in the midst of writing his re-introduction. Ratner calls it "a philosophical interpretation of the history of Western man." That is far too vague and too aloof in tone for me. I prefer to call it "a criticism of the course Western philosophy has taken in recent history." Even better might be "John Dewey's Own View of the Story of Philosophy and Related Matters," for it is narrative in form and it is also very personal in the sense of presenting without apology the story-teller's own reactions to the events being narrated.

Dewey's Story of Philosophy

In the briefest of retellings, the story goes like this: What we today call the Modern Age began somewhat abruptly about four hundred years ago with the emergence of several major scientific and geographical discoveries and with the concomitant revolution that took place in economic and political affairs. Dewey sums up the direction of those changes as being "from conformity to invention" and "from subjection to command" (LW1, 360). Experience, Dewey points out, was among the concepts whose character and function were dramatically transformed. As the result of experiments like those of Galileo, Dewey says, "The empirical became the experimental" (LW1, 335).

As dramatic and far-reaching in their consequences as many of those changes turned out to be, they did not manage to sweep the slate clean, not by a long shot. Indeed, they still have not done so, some four hundred years later. Old habits die hard. Out-moded ways of thinking persist in the midst of the modern age. They do so, Dewey explains, because "Revolutions in the formal organization of human relationships are much easier to effect than revolutions in the hearts and minds of men" (LW1, 336).

Among the most tenacious of those antiquated modes of feeling and thought, according to Dewey, has been the persistent search for what is eternal and immutable. Dewey looks upon that search as misguided. Yet he also sees it as expressing an almost irrepressible human yearning for stability in a world of change. Our only hope of satisfying that yearning, he believes, lies in our acting intelligently in the social and material world that constitutes empirical reality. Pinning our hopes on the efficacy of such action, having faith in the self-correcting nature of experience as guided by thought, is the true legacy of modernity.

Much of modern philosophy, Dewey believes, has been out of step with the spirit of the times. Instead of joining the move toward a more intelligently guided future, many philosophers have remained devoted to a search for the eternal and the immutable. Different groups of them have pursued that search in opposite directions. Those whom Dewey calls "rigoristic philosophers" have sought, through newly invented forms of logic, to establish a philosophical foundation on which science itself could rest secure. Dewey judges much of that new logic to be in "fly-blown condition." He finds "something outright comical" about the assumption that logic can provide the authority for such foundations. He likewise remarks on "the absurdity" of seeking foundations for science outside of the methods of knowing that have been experimentally tested and retested.

Those philosophers whom Dewey calls the "absolutistic super-rational moralists" have gone searching for the immutable and the eternal in the opposite direction (LW1, 356). They have joined ranks with "traditional supernaturalists" in locating the eternal in "the sacred realm of the moral, spiritual, and ideal" (LW1, 355) while at the same time denouncing the secular as the source of all that is morally lacking. There would be value in such a denunciation, Dewey goes on to say, if it were accompanied by an analysis of the actual conditions that need to be changed along with some notions of how to change them. Instead, however, the super-rational moralists, together with the traditional supernaturalists, have done little more than glorify the sacred at the expense of the secular.

Dewey's corrective to these conditions, as we have already seen in our two earlier chapters, calls for a philosophy that has abandoned the futile search for the eternal and the immutable in favor of maintaining a thorough and comprehensive interest in the culture at large. This would include an interest in the changes taking place in economic and political affairs as much as in those involving moral, aesthetic, and scientific matters. Indeed, it is with respect to the interdependence of those major forms of experience that philosophy may have the most interesting and helpful things to say.

Dewey illustrates that possibility nicely in an example drawn from economics. He shows how modern economists in their zeal to be "scientific" have been inspired by what he calls "a dehumanized conception of the nature of science" (LW1, 359). That conception is one that is limited to the techniques that scientists have found useful when dealing with physical subject matters from which "human (value) considerations were explicitly ruled out" (LW1, 359). But of course economics, which explicitly concerns the things humans value, cannot be stripped of such considerations without having its special character as a form of experience eviscerated. The scientistic pretensions of economics thus become farcical, much like those of a "rigoristic" philosophy.

This example also helps to dispel some of the misunderstanding that sometimes attaches to Dewey's enthusiastic endorsement of the so-called scientific method. That endorsement does not entail the recommendation that one lay aside human considerations when considering human affairs. To do so would be patently absurd. It entails, in fact, the exact opposite. It calls for a full consideration of all that is relevant and consequential in the making of all kinds of decisions. That includes bringing human considerations into the arena of deliberations in the physical sciences when circumstances require, as we have learned of late to do with increasing frequency.

Dewey begins the final section of his Re-introduction (final only in the sense that it is where his writing abruptly stops—he clearly had more to say) by calling attention to the "change of emotional tone" occurring over the course of his discussion. He began, he points out, on a note of optimism, employing the words of Lord Acton to herald an exhilarating prospect of change as the medieval world succumbs to the forces of modernity. That optimism weakens, however, as his story unfolds. By the time readers reach his description of the present they find themselves "confronted with a world literally torn more deeply and sharply apart than ever before since man appeared on earth" (LW1, 360).

That change of emotional tone has not been added for effect, Dewey insists. It is part of the story, a true change that has occurred over the years. It only becomes apparent, however, when we step back far enough "to report in generalized terms" on what has taken place (LW1, 360). Otherwise, such a shift might escape the attention of even those who live through it. Why so? Because "it takes time for events to disclose in which direction they are moving." Seen up close, they may seem to have no direction at all. One of philosphy's tasks is to disclose those features of human experience that can be detected only from afar. That is what Dewey means when he talks about reporting "in generalized terms what was going on."

Such language returns us to Dewey's image of the philosopher as mapmaker. It also calls to mind some of the things we have said about Dewey's image of the philosopher as cultural critic, as someone engaged in helping others disrobe intellectually. Dewey must have had such thoughts in mind himself at about this point in his labor of writing the Re-introduction, for in its next-to-the-last paragraph, which is where we now are in our review of it, he reverts explicitly to mapmaking imagery. He does so in explaining what the next section, which we now know he was never to write, is to contain.

> The persuasion that actuates the following section of this Re-Introduction is, then, that events of the present century, including positive and negative alike, taking accomplishments and the breakdowns together, indicate *the path to be followed* in order to arrive at *an awareness of the orbit of change-in-process* during the past four centuries or so (LW1, 360, emphasis added).

What I find striking about that sentence is the way it draws upon both forms of imagery (the mapmaker and the cultural critic) at the same time. The path to be followed is not one that leads to a physical destination. It leads instead to an intellectual endpoint, a form of awareness. Of what are we to become aware of on that path? Dewey continues,

> This path will enable us to observe with some effective degree of intellectual clarity the clogging, deflecting and distorting factors inherited from pre-scientific, pre-technological and pre-democratic conditions of living and knowing. In consequence, it will enable us to pursue with reasonable degree of confidence and resolution the orbit of change; having the advantage of sense of direction, the orbit will become clearer as it becomes increasingly unified (LW1, 360).

Here is how I would restate the contents of those two sentences as a pair of interlocking *if . . . then* propositions. *If* (condition 1) we could be given a clearer notion than we have at present of the general direction (the orbit) of the progressive changes taking place in Western society over the past several hundred years *and if, at the same time* (condition 2), we could be helped to see how old habits of thought and social practices presently retard or stand in the way of those changes, we *then* (as outcome) could pursue the latter with increased confidence and resolution. The task of philosophy, in Dewey's view, is to contribute to that end.

Dewey's final words on the subject (again, final only temporally and only with respect to this one document) reiterate his conviction about the centrality of the concept of experience in Western thought and about how its vicissitudes as a concept constitute a standing problem for philosophy. Yet it is not a concept to be explicated by philoso-

phers alone. In fact, their account of it may not be particularly trust-
worthy. Philosophers themselves need to consult other sources. Here
is the advice Dewey gives:

> I know of no more promising place from which to attempt to foreshadow
> the direction to be pursued by philosophy than to go back to the concern of
> the age (now drawing to a close) with experience. We must here view expe-
> rience not from the side of the stammering account given of it in philosophy
> but must see the new faith which found expression in our common tongue,
> our idiomatic speech as well as in the various disjointed because indepen-
> dent movements undertaken in pursuit of experience. Thus to see and grasp
> experience it is necessary to overcome the cultivated inability to see what is
> to be seen in the continuities displayed by what is in process and only by
> what is in process (LW1, 360).

What Dewey is saying is that the new faith in experience that marks
our age is not something we need go searching for in ponderous philosophic tomes. All we need do is look around. Its evidence is before us.
We can hear it in the way we talk. We can see it in the details of daily
life. We find its expression in the myriad ways in which we invite exploration and experimentation in so many facets of our lives. We observe it as well in our increased willingness to learn from others and
to share their experiences.

Yet there does seem to be some obstacle, Dewey calls it a "culti-
vated inability," that needs to be overcome if we are to see the evidence
of an increased faith in experience. Dewey speaks of it as an inability
"to see what is to be seen in the continuities displayed by what is in
process and only by what is in process." But what does that mean? The
phrase "the continuities displayed by what is in process" I find hard
to interpret. Also, why would anyone bother to *cultivate* an inability
to see such continuities? I can only wish that Dewey had said more.
Perhaps if he had gone on he might have made his meaning clear.

Such difficulties aside, where does Dewey's Re-Introduction leave
us insofar as an understanding of his philosophic method is concerned?
What does it tell us, if anything, about the direction he might have been
taking in his three successive attempts to address that subject? Here is
where it leaves me.

Dewey's historical overview of philosophy's shortcomings leaves
me wondering what a historian would make of the same set of events.
How would his or her account differ from Dewey's? If the answer is
"Not at all," then how are we to distinguish between the task of the

historian and that of the philosopher? The same question arises if we replace the word *historian* with *cultural critic*.

I suspect that Dewey's answer to both questions would have something to do with the level of generality at which philosophers, as opposed to historians and cultural critics, typically work. Philosophers supposedly reach higher for their generalizations than do either of the other two. Perhaps they are also less immersed in particularities as well, though such differences, if they exist at all, are no doubt relative at best.

Does it make any sense to draw distinctions among the three (again, only relatively) on the basis of their temporal fixations? Could we say that the historian tends to be fixated on the past, the cultural critic on the present, and the philosopher on the future? That would make too neat a division, I fear. Yet it does accommodate, at least crudely, Dewey's attraction to the metaphor of the mapmaker with his view from the mountain top. For it is toward the future that Dewey's gaze seems most intently drawn.

But such speculations do not advance our understanding of where Dewey was headed in his four attempts to introduce *Experience and Nature*. Perhaps, therefore, they are best delayed at least until we have finished examining the fourth of those attempts. For the present, we need only note that Dewey's lengthy Re-Introduction, begun almost twenty-five years after the original first chapter was written, has him pondering the impact of the intervening events on the use of *experience* as an all-encompassing term to stand for the overall subject matter of philosophy. In the process of weighing that impact, Dewey is led to report on attempts within philosophy itself to curtail the reference of the term, to "hold it down to an aspect that at its very best is but a highly specialized cross-section of experience" (LW1, 330). The cost of that curtailment, Dewey insists, has been the progressive isolation of philosophy from human affairs.

THE SECOND ATTEMPT AT A RE-INTRODUCTION

Dewey's second stab at re-introducing *Experience and Nature* is only eight paragraphs in length. It begins with the surprising announcement,

> Were I to write (or rewrite) *Experience and Nature* today I would entitle the book *Culture and Nature* and the treatment of specific subject-matters would be correspondingly modified (LW1, 361).

Why the change? Because, says Dewey, the "historical obstacles" that stood in the way of his use of *experience* have turned out to be insurmountable. He should have seen that from the start, he now admits, but he failed to do so. Meanwhile, thanks to advances in anthropology, the term *culture* has since expanded in its meaning so that it now stands for almost everything that *experience* once did. This means that *culture* is no longer in thrall of those, like Matthew Arnold, who would reserve its application to the tastes and habits of the socially elite. Therefore, the change is essentially linguistic rather than substantive.

What were the obstacles that stood in the way initially? Dewey does not bother to say. But he does say enough to convey the gist of what happened. Developments inside and outside of philosophy had the consequence of effectively identifying *experience* with "experiencing in the sense of the psychological." The *psychological* became established as "that which is intrinsically psychical, mental, private" (LW1, 362). Thus came to an end Dewey's almost lifelong crusade to have *experience* serve as the term that would stand for the inclusive subject matter of philosophy. His effort was foiled almost before it began.

Dewey's choice of the word *culture* to replace *experience* rested on what he had come to understand about the way leading anthropologists of his day were using the term, Bronislaw Malinowski being the outstanding example.

On the opening page of his seminal article "Culture," which appeared in the 1931 edition of *The Encyclopedia of the Social Sciences*, Malinowski proclaimed that "culture comprises inherited artifacts, goods, technical processes, ideas, habits, values" (p. 621). He also opined that "Social organization [which heretofore had been the primary focus of anthropological investigations] cannot be really understood except as a part of culture" (p. 621). Dewey could not have agreed more. He quoted both statements verbatim. He also quoted with obvious approval five other fragments culled from the opening pages of Malinowski's article. The last declared: "Culture is *at the same time* psychological and collective" (LW1, 364). The emphasis was Dewey's own. He did not want the significance of that simultaneity to be overlooked. The underlining of those four words constituted Dewey's final gesture in his fourth attempt to introduce *Experience and Nature* to a new generation of readers. His writing stops there.

What if he had gone on? Where might his proposed substitution of *culture* for *experience* have taken him? Would it have changed his conception of philosophy's task? Might he have been on his way to recommending a new hybridization of disciplines, a blending that might one day be worthy of being called *cultural philosophy* or *philosophical anthropology*? I think not, although a move in that general direction looks to be afoot in certain quarters today.[3]

What Dewey found to be attractive about the notion of experience in the first place was its breadth of coverage. As he wanted the term used, it was to stand for everything experienced as well as for the process of experiencing. When he finally came to accept the futility of getting others to use the term in that way, he turned to the notion of culture instead. His goal, however, had not changed. He was still searching for a linguistic expression that would stand for the comprehensiveness of philosophy's subject matter. Dewey called that comprehensiveness "philosophy's singular distinction" (LW1, 362).

Whether he was right about the singularity of that distinction is called into question by Clifford Geertz's remarks in his Introduction to a recent collection of his own essays:

> As befits two disciplines, neither of which is clearly defined and both of which address themselves to the whole of human life and thought, anthropology and philosophy are more than a little suspicious of one another. The anxiety that comes with a combination of a diffuse and miscellaneous academic identity and an ambition to connect just about everything with everything else and get, thereby, to the bottom of things leaves both of them unsure as to which of them should be doing what. It is not that their borders overlap, it is that they have no borders anyone can, with any assurance, draw. It is not that their interests diverge, it is that nothing, apparently, is alien to either of them (2000, ix).

If, as Geertz suggests, both anthropology and philosophy "address themselves to the whole of human life and thought" and if "nothing . . . is alien to either of them," it then cannot be that comprehensiveness of subject matter is philosophy's *singular* distinction. It has to be a distinction shared with at least one other discipline.

Moreover, it is not very hard to imagine a historian making a similiar claim on behalf of history. History too, it would seem, addresses the whole of human life and thought. Dewey's use of the quotation from Lord Acton's address at the start of the Re-Introduction to *Experience and Nature* helps to substantiate such a claim, making it seem quite plausible.

Yet philosophers are certainly not anthropologists, most everyone would agree, even though a few individuals may answer to both designations. Nor are philosophers historians, save again for rare exceptions. But if not in the comprehensiveness of its subject matter, wherein, then, lies philosophy's distinctiveness?

The answer to that question seems almost too obvious to put into words. In the case of anthropology, the chief difference is that anthropologists are mainly interested in cultures other than their own, whereas philosophers are not. Crudely put, anthropologists take field trips; philosophers, for the most part, stay home.[4]

With respect to the discipline of history, the chief difference seems to be that historians are mainly focused on past events, whereas philosophers may be interested in the past but usually only secondarily. If the difference between the interests of anthropologists and philosophers is principally spatial or geographical, that between historians and philosophers is principally temporal.

Of course the features that differentiate the three disciplines do not stop there by any means, as we all well know. Most anthropologists, for example, think of themselves as social scientists, and so do many historians; philosophers, as a rule, do not. This means, among other things, that anthropologists and historians are far more interested than philosophers in the compilation of individual items of information and in the discovery of new facts about the world (past or present). It also means that usually they are more caught up in technical issues having to do with data-gathering procedures, quantitative methods, statistical analysis, and so forth.

Are anthropologists and historians as a rule less judgmental than philosophers in outlook? That is a somewhat harder distinction to make and maintain, I would say, yet if we are to stay within a Deweyan perspective on the philosopher's task, I think we would have to entertain such a possibility. Dewey's philosopher is openly committed to the goal of social betterment through the continued criticism of ongoing social practices and cultural traditions. Philosophy for Dewey is clearly a moral endeavor. I can easily imagine his arguing that the same is true of anthropology and history, at least in the long run. Yet I am not sure that most anthropologists and historians would readily agree. Therein may lie yet another distinction.

This brief exercise in the cataloging of a few of the major differences between and among anthropologists, historians, and philosophers calls attention to the fact that the distinctiveness of philosophy involves far more than the comprehensiveness of its subject matter, which may not be so distinctive after all. Differences of goals, purposes, interests, techniques, values, and more seem to be involved. None of those differences by itself seems sufficient to capture the distinctiveness of any of the three disciplines.

This leads to the thought that perhaps the term *philosophic method*, as Dewey uses it in *Experience and Nature*, bears too much weight. As it appears there, the term stands for all that makes philosophy unique, all that separates it from other forms of activity. What if that weight were distributed differently?

Suppose we were to think of philosophy as something like *a practice* or *a tradition*, or even, to interject a Wittgensteinian term, *a form of life*. Would not that be more accommodating overall? For when Dewey talks about things like the philosopher's faith in experience or when he extols the virtue of remaining moored in the stuff of everyday life as starting place and terminus, he certainly seems to be going far beyond anything that could properly be called method.

Perhaps if we broadened our conception of what Dewey is calling philosophic method, putting another term in its place, we might also be led to deal more imaginatively than we yet have done with his figurative language—his penchant for talking about the philosopher as mapmaker and as someone who invites others to disrobe intellectually. Perhaps too we could then better come to terms with the emotionality of Dewey's writing, his impatience with philosophers who yearn to escape from the world of experience, his clear delight in the transient joys of life, his unhappiness in the face of current social conditions, his optimistic hope for a better future.

Yet we must take care not to abandon the idea of method too quickly. What Dewey calls philosophic method may not be reducible to a step-by-step procedure, but neither is it entirely devoid of methodological relevance. It still refers to a way of doing things. We must not lose sight of how it does manage to convey a sense of direction, a crude notion of how philosophical reflection should proceed. In the next chapter I attempt to bring out the significance of methodological implications by focusing on the figural aspects of Dewey's view of philosophy.

CHAPTER 4

Picturing the Philosopher's Task

A few months after his 90th birthday had been celebrated, he [Dewey] remarked, "Only in the last two years have I come to see the real drift and hang of the various positions I have taken."
—Sidney Hook, in Sidney Morgenbesser,
Dewey and His Critics, 1977, 9

Like formless fog on aimless cruise
Over fens when pallid waters ooze
Wand'ring I drift—

But look! Upon the leaden sky—
Whereto my thoughts, aweary, scarce may fly
A gleam, a rift—

Now to a sweet and sunlit land,
By heaven's own blue in peace o'erspanned,
I come, swift, swift—
—John Dewey, *The Poems of John Dewey,* 1977, 77–78

I have been engaged by means of published writings in developing the essentials of my present philosophical views for at least thirty-five years. . . . Inconsistencies and shifts have taken place; the most I can claim is that I have moved fairly steadily in one direction.
—John Dewey, in Paul Arthur Schilpp, *The Philosophy of John Dewey,*
1939, 520

DEWEY'S USE OF FIGURATIVE LANGUAGE

Sidney Hook's recollection of Dewey's comment about his own insight into where he had been going intellectually has always fascinated me. Could it be true that it was not until Dewey was close to ninety that he came to see "the real drift and hang" of the positions he had taken? "What took him so long?" one wonders, and "What in particular did he finally come to see?"

The reason I find that last question so compelling is that something very much like it was uppermost in my mind when I began the writing of this book. What got me started, readers will recall, was my puzzling over the fact of Dewey's repeated efforts to introduce *Experience and Nature* to its successive audiences of readers. I wondered at the time why he kept returning to the task. I suspected his doing so might have something to do with the overall direction his thought was taking during the final phase of his life. I pictured him as someone who was trying again and again to get something right, to hit the bull's-eye dead center, as the saying goes. I decided to try to find out what that "something" was. This book is the result of that effort. Small wonder, therefore, that I find Dewey's comment to Hook captivating.

There is another reason, however, for my attraction to Hook's account. Dewey's colorful language added to its appeal. The nautical phrase "drift and hang" called to mind the image of a ship under sail. The word "positions" added to the picture. It made me think of sextants and charts and other navigational devices.

Dewey's use of nautical imagery to describe his philosophical excursions is actually not uncommon. He frequently drew upon such figurative language in a number of poems he wrote when he was fifty and beyond.[1] A fairly typical example appears above, just below the Sidney Hook anecdote. The poem portrays the plight of a sailor (ostensibly the poet himself) who discovers himself adrift at the start but finds his way at last.[2] That it turns out to be the poet's "thoughts" that are cruising aimlessly around and "scarce may fly" underscores the figurative nature of what is being said.

Dewey not only drew on imagery having to do with sea travel when discussing his work as a philosopher; he also employed several other figures of speech that refer to physical movement and geographical positioning of one kind or another. He often talked about the paths and routes the philosopher must take, for example. He also, as we have seen, repeatedly compared the work of the philosopher to that of a mapmaker or field guide. The mapmaker simile is perhaps the most fully elaborated of all his figurations.

What I find especially noteworthy about the use of such language is how naturally it fits the situation. It hardly seems figurative at all. Instead, it reads almost like a literal description of what philosophers do.

Mindful of how readily such figurative devices fit our talk about what philosophers do, I recall how perfectly natural it seemed to me at the start of my own investigation to raise the question about the direction in which Dewey was headed in his four attempts to introduce *Experience and Nature*. "Where was he going?" I wondered back then. Why did I think of him as "going" somewhere? Simply because that has been and remains our most common way of speaking about such matters.

But that easy answer to why we employ such terminology skirts what needs addressing, which is the role that such common ways of speaking might play in actually *shaping* the way we think about something rather than neutrally describing it. It overlooks the warning implicit in what Wittgenstein and a host of others have taught us during the latter half of the last century about the consequences of being in the grip of mental pictures that give rise to false problems and faulty ways of thinking. It fails, in other words, to give adequate attention to the figurative nature of such language and to the good or evil that may be a consequence of its use.

I seek to address that oversight in this chapter by taking a protracted look at Dewey's use of figurative language. I am interested in particular in his recurrent reliance on imagery involving mapmaking and sea travel when describing the work of philosophy. Why does he seem drawn to the image of the philosopher as either a mapmaker or a sea traveler? Can one envision just any philosopher of Dewey's day—Bertrand Russell, let's say, or Carnap or Whitehead—making use of either of those images? I for one have difficulty doing so.[3] Both images seem almost custom-made for Dewey. Why might that be so? Is the choice just one of personal predilection? Or might something more be involved, something having to do with the particular kind of philosophy that Dewey is seeking to establish as the norm?

To explore the latter possibility I first call attention to three prominent features of Dewey's philosophical position. I couch those features in the form of three major commitments that Dewey appears to have held, each of them dealing with how philosophers should go about their work. I then turn to the various ways in which each of those commitments either resists or lends itself to figural portrayal.

DEWEY'S THREE PHILOSOPHICAL COMMITMENTS

The trio of beliefs under discussion comprise the following:

1. Philosophy is an avowedly empirical endeavor; its Deweyan practitioner not only harbors no ambition to transcend experience but explicitly rejects the possibility of anyone's doing so.
2. Philosophy is melioristic in intent; it aims to be of value not just to philosophers but to the society at large.
3. Philosophy is an intellectual activity that traffics in abstractions yet remains inextricably entangled in ordinary affairs.

   I do not claim that these three doctrines adequately cover all that Dewey believes about how philosophy should be conducted. Nor am I saying that they are the only three principles that could be extracted from all that Dewey says about philosophy in *Experience and Nature*. Yet I do believe each of them captures an essential aspect of his deepest convictions. I select these in particular, as has been said, because of the way they either resist or lend themselves to certain figural depictions of the philosopher's task. After trying to make some of those connections explicit, I turn to the image of the philosopher as mapmaker and then to some of Dewey's nautical imagery in order to show how those particular tropes relate in particular ways to the potential for figuration implicit in the second and third of Dewey's three key beliefs.

1. Philosophy as an Empirical Endeavor

Philosophy is an avowedly empirical endeavor; its Deweyan practitioner not only harbors no ambition to transcend experience but explicitly rejects the possibility of anyone's doing so. This conviction stands so prominently in the forefront of Dewey's thought that it deserves pride of place. Dewey uses the word *empirical* frequently in *Experience and Nature,* as we know. He labels his own view of philosophy "empirical naturalism." Yet there is something odd about Dewey's use of that term. For there is a sense in which it does not really distinguish Dewey's way of working from that of any other philosopher. In his heart of hearts Dewey is convinced that when viewed non-ideologically all philosophies are empirical. They must be. There is nothing else for them to be.

They are empirical in the sense of being occurrences within an empirical world, a world of objects and events, physical and ideational, among which they themselves are entities. Thus even those philosophers whom Dewey criticizes for being nonempirical—idealists, for example—go about their business *empirically*. They have no choice but to do so. They may not *espouse* empiricism ideologically, true enough, which means they are not *avowed* empiricists, like Dewey, but they still live their lives and dream their dreams in a thoroughly empirical world. Thus Dewey uses terms like *empirical* and *empiricism* a bit like political campaign buttons. They stand as public declarations of his commitment to a position that he is prepared to defend against rival claims. For him to call his opponents "non-empirical" is not just to describe their position but to evaluate it. Implicitly, it is to criticize them.

This difference between the avowal and the nonavowal of empiricism is crucial for Dewey. It also has very important consequences for the ways in which the goals of philosophy are depicted, either pictorially or with other kinds of figurative language. To see why that is so we need return briefly to Dewey's conception of experience.

Near the start of the revised version of Chapter 1 of *Experience and Nature* Dewey reminded his readers that

> It is not experience which is experienced, but nature—stones, plants, animals, diseases, health, temperature, electricity, and so on. Things interacting in certain ways *are* experience, they are what is experienced (LW1, 12).

A few pages further on he adds to that list a number of nonphysical objects and events:

> The possibilities present in imagination that are not found in observation, are something to be taken into account. . . . So are all the phenomena of magic, myth, politics, painting, and penitentiaries (LW1, 27).

These too, in other words, are among what is experienced.

Yet the stricture of Dewey's opening clause remains: The one thing we do not experience is experience itself. But at the same time we speak of experience in general, independent of this or that object or event that happens to be experienced. Another way of putting it would be to say that we *thematize* experience. In so doing we may even go so far as to *objectify* it. We do this, in part, by making use of the pronoun *it*. We may even *picture* experience as having certain properties much like physical objects. We took note above of Dewey's finding plenty of room for magic, myths, and politics in his empirical world.

But here is where the danger of false pictures begins to creep in. For to conceive of experience in spatial terms, as a kind of container within which objects and events are located, is to invite thinking of it as something having an "inside" and an "outside." It is as though one could look upon experience "sideways," so to speak, visually imagining the empty space surrounding it. Under the sway of such a picture one is but a short step from wondering how to penetrate those boundaries and how to occupy that space. We fantasize about what it would be like to experience what lies on the "other side" of experience.

But that possibility is precisely what Dewey's empiricism rejects. Experience cannot be viewed "sideways," save mythically, and therefore from a perspective that is decidedly nonempirical. For to view experience "sideways" would presuppose that one had already penetrated its "boundaries" and was viewing it from a position—the legendary Archimedean point—that no human could possibly occupy. The poet Wallace Stevens entertains such a possibility in a poem entitled "The Plain Sense of Things." He looks upon the leafless trees in winter as offering a glimpse of what it would be like to look upon the world absent the power of being able to see it through human eyes. But then he realizes that "the absence of imagination had/ Itself to be imagined." "Ditto experience," Dewey would say. "The absence of experience has itself to be experienced."

Experience, for Dewey, has no boundaries. It encompasses what some might call *The All*, which would include both background and foreground, both perceiver and perceived, both dream and reality. The objects and events we identify as having been experienced reside within an all-enveloping matrix—variously referred to by some philosophers with capitalized nouns, such as *World*, *Nature*, *Environment*, *Situation*—whose "horizons" (another familiar figurative device for conveying the notion of a nonexistent boundary) can be altered and expanded but never exceeded. Searching for a comparison, I can think of no modern philosophical notion closer to Dewey's all-embracing conception of experience than the one that Martin Heidegger speaks of as *Being* in his now classic treatise, *Being and Time* (1962).[4]

The fact that false or mythical portrayals of experience are empirically meaningless does not affect their status as portrayals. False pictures remain pictures all the same. Nor does it mean that because they are merely pictures, and false ones at that, they have no useful function. The dream of transcending experience has been around for millennia and is not likely to go away even should all of humanity reach the point of no longer taking it seriously as an empirical possibility. Indeed, despite his avowed empiricism, Dewey himself clandestinely indulged in such imaginings from time to time. We find him doing so on more than one occasion in his poetry, most of which, we will recall, he did not intend to share with others.

The form that indulgence takes in his poems is one of offering prayerful entreaties that seemingly express a belief in the existence of a divine Being and in the capacity of prayer to penetrate the realm of human experience and reach the Great Beyond. Yet side by side with such entreaties are other poems contradicting such a possibility and expressing an impatience with those who cling to such beliefs. In one such poem he speaks almost with bravado of the courage it takes to proceed through life on one's own, absent all hope of divine intervention and guidance. He encourages others to do the same.

> *Driven forever our uncaptained ship*
> *As portless as a bobbing chip.*
> *Let souls dispirited and craven*
> *Whine for some rewarding haven,*
>
> *Plumb the fathomless, weigh the anchor*
> *Lower sails in puny rancor—*
> *For us the salty sea, th'untamed wind:—*
> *Enslaved and free, both seek their kind.*
> *(1977, 54)*

Yet such bravado has its limits, as becomes clear in adjacent poems. The following, for example, is from a poem in which the poet confronts the realization of life's finitude. It begins with the question, "Is this the end?" spoken as though the poet were almost taken by surprise by the realization that time is running out. After eight lines of complaint about being caught between a past of fleeting memories and a future of defeated hopes, the poet entreats,

> *Great God, I thee implore*
> *A little help to lend:—*
> *I do not ask for much,*
> *A little space in which to move,*

> *To reach, perchance to touch;*
> *A little time in which to love;*
> *A little hope that things which were*
> *Again may living stir—*
> *A future with an op'ning door:*
> *Dear God, I ask no more*
> *Than that these bonds may rend,*
> *And leave me free as before.*
> *(1977, 7)*

It thus seems that during moments of despair, of which he seems to have had a fair share during the period of his life when he was writing poetry, Dewey was not above crying out for help to an otherworldly God in whose literal existence he did not actually believe. In the light of Dewey's avowed empiricism, to which he was fully committed long before writing those lines, some might call Dewey's cries for help hypocritical. I am reluctant to do so, however, for I do not believe that Dewey was trying to pass himself off to others as being a "true believer." Nor do I believe that he was trying to fool himself.

Instead, I read such poems of Dewey as embodying emotional truths, as containing figurative expressions of how he felt at a time presumably close to when the poem was written (cf. Wordsworth's "emotions recollected in tranquility"). They are not to be read as a set of statements to be taken literally *even as gestures.* But neither are they to be treated dismissively as *mere* figures of speech. They lie between or beyond fiction and fact and in so doing they either blur the distinction or fall outside its range of application. They are a part of what Wallace Stevens refers to as "a supreme fiction," which is the term he applies to poetry. He also calls it a "more than rational distortion" and "the fiction that results from feeling" (1990b, 233). He elsewhere explains,

> The relation of art to life is of the first importance especially in a skeptical age since, in the absence of a belief in God, the mind turns to its own creations and examines them, not alone from the aesthetic point of view, but for what they reveal, for what they validate and invalidate, for the support that they give (1990a, 186).

The "fictions" that Stevens is referring to in that passage are, as he says, the mind's own creations, such as the many fictional figures that populate his own poetry. There is nothing to prevent one, however, from making use of conventional figures, including that of God Himself, for the same set of purposes. As Stevens goes on to say,

> The final belief is to believe in a fiction, which you know to be a fiction, there being nothing else. The exquisite truth is to know that it is a fiction and that you believe in it willingly (1990a, 189).

Can one believe in a fiction, knowing it to be a fiction? I think Dewey would have trouble with that idea, though I may be doing him an injustice in saying so. To claim that there is "nothing else" but fiction seems to do away entirely with the distinction between fact and fiction, a separation that I suspect Dewey would want to retain and call upon for certain purposes. At the same time I think he would be receptive to the idea that the distinction is by no means universally applicable and that there are times when it makes no sense to draw the distinction, either because it is irrelevant to the circumstances or because it is just plain impossible to tease truth and fiction apart even when it would be helpful to do so. Dewey describes one of those situations in yet another of his poems. In the lines to follow he laments his inability to discriminate between what he calls "mimic passions" and the real McCoy. He blames the situation in part on his reading of fiction and romantic literature during his youth. He curses having done so.

> *Damn fiction, damn romance.*
> *Since I have read, I shall never know*
> *Whether in an ancient mirror I see prance*
> *Before me mimic passions in a row,*
> *Or if they are authentic heaven and hell.*

But he also realizes that the problem is not just one of having read too much romantic fiction. For he goes on,

> *Moreover, no one can ever tell.*
> *For we are more than simple brute*
> *Only in that there have entered into us*
> *The thoughts of others which taking root*
> *Have bred the plant and seed whose surplus,*
> *Saved from waste, is called ourselves.*
> *(1977, 16)*

The thought expressed in those lines ties to Dewey's avowal of empiricism in the following way. The meanings we attach to objects and events come to us initially from the thoughts and actions of others. We inhabit from the very beginning a meaningful social world. We do not enter experience from the outside. We are in it from the start.

The meanings we encounter, most of them inherited, change as we develop, true enough, yet we can never totally rid ourselves of our cultural heritage, nor would we want to even if we could. This is why Dewey recommends a method of cultural criticism that allows us to examine that heritage a piece at a time, shedding it like an outer garment that upon examination we may wish to discard or perhaps resume wearing.

The fact that in our customary ways of speaking we do not always distinguish between the literal and the figurative uses of language is neither good nor bad. It depends on the consequences of making or not making those distinctions. What Dewey objected to about the often unverbalized picture of experience that held many of his fellow philosophers in thrall was not just that it was false or logically inconceivable but that, when taken literally and therefore acted upon, it had untoward consequences. It led to unreasonable expectations. It spurred fruitless investigations. It reinforced damaging social distinctions.

The thought of such consequences returns us to the question raised at the start of this chapter, which is whether certain forms of figuration are better suited than others to describing certain ways of doing philosophy. In particular we are interested in the unique suitability of Dewey's own use of figural language. We must delay exploring that question further, however, until we have re-introduced the two remaining core beliefs.

2. Philosophy as Melioristic in Intent

Philosophy is melioristic in intent; it aims to be of value not solely to philosophers but to the society at large. If Dewey's opposition to absolute idealism and absolute realism might be said to express the negative side of his avowed empiricism, its positive side must surely find expression in his wholehearted advocacy of social reform and in his insistence that philosophy contribute to that reform by directing its investigations to bear upon issues of concern to the society at large. Operationally, this conviction is at one with the related notion that philosophy has no subject matter of its own. Its province is all of experience.

What that conviction means figuratively is that the philosopher is free to move about, freer, presumably, than many other theoreticians or specialists whose activities are confined to a single discipline or to one or another "field" of study or "area" of investigation. It also means, however, that the philosopher's choice of what to study or, in figurative terms, of what "area" to investigate, is at least partially determined by what the society as a whole takes to be problematic.

The imagery that lends itself most easily to a depiction of that state of affairs involves physical movement interspersed with periods of relatively stationary labor. The movement would presumably traverse a surface demarcated by "regions" defined by specific subject matter or clusters of problems. The periods of relatively stationary activity would constitute work on a single problem. Dewey, as we have seen, discursively sketches such a program of activity in his discussion of *forms* of experience. He lists a half dozen or so such forms, including political, aesthetic, religious, and scientific experience, offering them as potential places for philosophical inquiry to begin. He leaves open the question of how the philosopher is to select from among the choices available. Presumably personal predilections and contingent conditions would determine that outcome.

Do those conditions implicitly suggest that the "itinerant" philosopher might often be quite uncertain about what direction to take once she had finished a particular investigation? Considered solely as possible contingencies that might be faced singly, perhaps not, yet it would not be hard to imagine circumstances that would easily arouse such uncertainty. Competing targets of investigation would be one such circumstance. Indeed, absent a clear-cut criterion for deciding what to study next, one might readily imagine that some residual doubt about the choice one has made may well hover for quite some time on the edge of awareness.

Another figural aspect having to do with the social value of philosophy concerns the philosopher's audience. To whom do we imagine the philosopher is speaking? A partial answer to that question is clearly implied in the commitment itself, which certainly suggests that whoever the audience might be, it does not consist solely of other philosophers. Dewey does not prohibit philosophers from speaking among themselves and even doing so in language that at times becomes quite technical and obscure to outsiders. He certainly did that himself on occasion. Yet he insists that they study problems of consequence to the society at large, which means addressing audiences of nonspecialists from time to time, perhaps even much of the time.

How do we picture the sharing of that responsibility among philosophers? Does Dewey's commitment to social melioration imply that all philosophers must address nonspecialists, or is it that only some of them need do so? Also, how great must we imagine the difference to be between the Deweyan philosopher and her audience? And of what does that difference consist? Presumably, if we wanted to represent the relationship between the philosopher and her audience spatially, we might picture the philosopher as talking "down" to her audience, though not "down" in a pejorative sense. But then, in what sense?

That final question provides a natural segue to the third of Dewey's three commitments.

3. Philosophy as an Intellectual Activity Entangled in Practical Affairs

Philosophy is an intellectual activity that traffics in abstractions yet remains inextricably entangled in ordinary affairs. This is another way of expressing philosophy's social commitment, but here the emphasis is on what happens within a single investigation rather than on the movement from one investigation to another. The figurative imagery especially suited to this commitment is also one of journeying, but in a far more circumscribed manner than that involving movement from field to field. It entails, above all, the notion of departing from and returning to more or less the same place.

The point of departure is the world of practical affairs, which is also the locus of return. The journey, in other words, is always a round trip. If practical affairs constitute both the starting point and the terminus of the philosophic journey, the furthest it travels away from that destination—its apogee, so to speak—lies somewhere in a region often referred to as "the heights of abstraction." The word *heights* tells us something else about the figural representation of the journey. In geometric terms the trip is basically vertical rather than horizontal. It involves ascending and then descending.

Another aspect of the vertical character of the journey deserves special mention. The natural proclivity of the philosopher, Dewey points out on several occasions, is to move in the direction of increasingly abstract expression. Abstract language, one might almost say, is the philosopher's metier. It comes close to being philosophy's distinguishing feature.[5] Yet, Dewey warns, as much as philosophers enjoy trafficking in abstraction, their doing so also has its drawbacks. The danger is that the philosopher so inclined may become so habituated to the rarefied discourse of philosophy and so engrossed in its manipulations that she would prefer to continue doing that. She no longer is willing to turn her thoughts back to the harsh complexities of ordinary affairs. Indeed, there are some philosophers, Dewey further points out, who avoid those complexities from the start. Instead of beginning with a problem of concern to the society at large, they plunge at once into matters of interest solely to a small coterie of their fellow philosophers (those specializing in the subtleties of formal logic would be an example) without bothering to consider the social benefits that might or might not flow from such an activity.

That picture of traversing an eliptical course from one destination to another and then back again is of course not limited in its application to philosophers alone but is familiarly applied in many different contexts. We find it commonly used, for example, to characterize all forms of inquiry, especially inquiry of the most advanced kind, such as that undertaken by scientists. Indeed, it is precisely the notoriety of the latter application that leaves Dewey puzzled. He seemingly cannot understand why more philosphers do not follow the same general precepts that have been shown to work so well in the field of science. Instead, too many philosophers remain cut off completely from the world of practical affairs. They either fail to test their ideas by returning to their starting place and trying to apply them or, worse yet, never launch their investigations from such starting places to begin with.

Dewey's apparent puzzlement on this point calls for clarification. If, indeed, all of inquiry can be aptly characterized by the picture of a cyclic movement from problem to proposed solution and back again (or some conventional variant of that formula), it must then be the case that even philosophers who never make the return trip that Dewey endorses—that is, from the world of practical affairs to the world of theory and back again—but who do nonetheless continue to think and write productively about philosophic matters are still traversing (figuratively of course) an elliptical path from problem ("How do I think about this question? How do I finish this sentence or this paragraph?") to proposed solution ("Is it possible that . . . ? Maybe I should then say . . . ") and back again. What Dewey is criticizing therefore is not a failure on the part of many philosophers to follow the basic rules of inquiry, although it sometimes sounds as though that was his complaint. His real objection focuses on where they begin and end their investigations. He criticizes them doubly: for not starting with ordinary affairs and for not ending with them. The criticism, in other words, is about their failure to fulfill a moral obligation to society, not about any mechanical or technical shortcomings they may have as investigators.

For those philosophers who seek to follow Dewey's precepts about the social obligations of philosophy and how to fulfill them, the round-trip journey from practical affairs to theory and back again often turns out to be surprisingly difficult. Dewey warns that such may be the case. He blames the nature of experience for that state of affairs. Experience, he explains, is "Protean; a thing of moods and tenses. To seize and report on it is the task of an artist as well as of an informed technician" (LW1, 367). He adds that the approach he is advocating calls for "unusual candor and patience" (LW1, 367).

All of that may be true, but is that explanation sufficient? I think not. I suspect there may be more to it than that. I wonder, in fact, whether part of the difficulty may be traced to the pictorial representation implicit in Dewey's third commitment.

To treat theory and practice as spatially separate locations that are "worlds apart" awaiting to be joined by some kind of arduous journey is of course to objectify them, thereby assigning them properties akin to those of physical objects. But of course there is no place called *theory* and none called *practice*. The same applies, naturally enough, to the companion terms *practical affairs* and *the heights of abstraction*. The imagery further implies that when one *leaves* practice one actually *departs* from something, severing one's connections with it. Ditto the state of affairs implied in moving in the other direction. But again, those are not descriptions of what actually happens or what *must* happen. There is nothing to prevent the theoretician from thinking about practical affairs (other than her own) while theorizing. Nor is there anything to prevent the practitioner from reflecting (theorizing) on what she is doing, even while doing it.

But why should such a false picture (assuming it to be so) add to the difficulty of either person? It could do so by needlessly exaggerating the distinction between one way of thinking and the other. So long as theory and practice are seen as worlds apart, they are that much more likely to remain so.

This is not to say that the elimination of a false mental picture is all that stands in the way of easy commerce on the pathways of thought, if we dare continue to think of them as *pathways*. Dewey is surely right about the continuing need for both artistry and technique in traversing such a course. The way likely remains difficult, even with false pictures laid aside.

What about doing away with *all* pictorial representations of the philosopher at work, including all analogies to other forms of activity? Aren't they all false, simply by virtue of their being figurative in nature?

Could we do so if we wished? I am not sure we could. I suspect there may be no way of talking about what philosophers do without resorting sooner or later to some kind of figurative expression to put such ideas across. But that conjecture aside, I also see some distinct advantages in retaining certain of those figurative depictions, especially those that offer an idealized image of what one would like to see philosophers doing, which are the kind of images that we have mostly been considering here. Are they all false, simply by virtue of being figurative? Yes and no. They certainly do not realistically depict the philosopher's lived experience. But they do convey some important truths about that experience all the same. They do other things as well.

They simplify, the way slogans and mottos simplify. They provide us with handy reminders of things we already know but conveniently neglect from time to time.

This is not to say that many or all of Dewey's figurations of philosophy are best seen as pictorial slogans or mottos of some kind. But it is to suggest that they often have a function akin to such devices, especially for those of his readers who share his commitment to a philosophy that seeks to make a difference in how people live their lives.

Let us now return, as promised, to two of Dewey's favorite tropes, each depicting very different aspects of the philosopher's task. We take up first his repeated references to maps and mapmaking. Following that, we examine his use of nautical imagery.

THE PHILOSOPHER AS MAPMAKER

To refresh our memory of how Dewey makes use of this figural device, let us reexamine several examples, beginning with its introduction near the close of the original first chapter.

> The empirical method points out when and where and how things of a designated description have been arrived at. It places before others *a map of*

> the road that has been travelled; they may accordingly, if they will, *re-travel the road* to *inspect the landscape* for themselves (LW1, 389, emphasis added).

Here is the same image in a slightly different guise in the revised first chapter. He is speaking about how scientists go about their work.

> Well, *they define or lay out a path* by which return to experienced things is of such a sort that the meaning, the significant content, of what is experienced gains an enriched and expanded force *because of the path* or method by which it was reached. Directly, in immediate contact it may be just what it was before—hard, colored, odorous, etc. But when the secondary objects, *the refined objects, are employed as a method or road for coming at them,* these qualities cease to be isolated details; they get the meaning contained in a whole system of related objects; they are rendered continuous with the rest of nature and take on the import of the things they are now seen to be continuous with. The phenomena observed in the eclipse tested and, as far as they went, confirmed Einstein's theory of deflection of light by mass. But that is far from being the whole story. The phenomena themselves got a far-reaching significance they did not previously have. Perhaps they would not even have been noticed *if the theory had not been employed as a guide or road to observation of them* (LW1, 16, emphasis added).

And here it is, once more, in the Re-introduction, written twenty years later.

> The persuasion that actuates the following section of this Re-Introduction is, then, that events of the present century, including positive and negative alike, taking accomplishments and the breakdowns together, indicate *the path to be followed* in order to arrive at *an awareness of the orbit of change-in-process* during the past four centuries or so. *This path will enable us to observe* with some effective degree of intellectual clarity the clogging, deflecting and distorting factors inherited from pre-scientific, pre-technological and pre-democratic conditions of living and knowing. In consequence, *it will enable us to pursue* with reasonable degree of confidence and resolution *the orbit of change;* having the advantage of *sense of direction, the orbit will become clearer* as it becomes increasingly unified (LW1, 360, emphasis added).

Finally, toward the very end of *Experience and Nature,* Dewey calls his variant of metaphysics, which refers to the generic traits manifested by existences of all kinds, "*a ground-map* of the province of criticism, establishing base lines to be employed in more intricate triangulations" (LW1, 309, emphasis added).

The first thing to ask about those examples is how they give expression to the three philosophical commitments that we have been examining in this chapter. I see them as doing so in several ways.[6]

The mapmaker imagery helps to concretize his commitment to empiricism. Makers of maps gaze upon the physical world. They look out on existing conditions. They focus on the here and now. Instead of trying to escape the bonds of experience, as idle dreamers might, they are content with describing things as they are.

Yet the view mapmakers offer cannot be called ordinary or close at hand. Rather, it is severely abstract, like that of Dewey's philosopher. Their vantage point is from afar, so distant, in fact, that it often cannot be accommodated in one sweeping gaze. Instead, it requires repeated viewings, not even from one point alone but from several. The successive images gained from such multiple vantage points combine to form a single view. The perspective sought in Dewey's Re-Introduction (as shown in the third of the above quotations) broadens sufficiently to trace the "orbit" of four centuries of history.

The type of map that Dewey most often refers to, however, is far humbler than the view that spans centuries. More often it resembles a road map of a kind that travelers routinely rely upon to reach their destination. The obvious usefulness of such devices perfectly fits Dewey's commitment to philosophy as a form of social service, a way of helping others.

As an aside, I must add that I also sense something decidedly American about Dewey's reliance on the mapmaker imagery. To me it hints of those qualities of exploration and adventure that one commonly associates with the period of westward expansion in this country. When I try to imagine Dewey's mapmaker, I see him in my mind's eye gazing out (westward, of course) from atop a high mountain, looking across a broad expanse, noting those features that signal the best route to follow. [7]

In sum, the imagery of maps and mapmaking nicely fits Dewey's three philosophical commitments. It is, to be sure, heroic in cast. It portrays the philosopher as a leader, pathfinder, and guide. It credits him with having keen vision but not with the power to see beyond the horizon. He is a Moses who leads the way but not one who talks with God.

Does the image mislead as well as inspire? That would depend on how literally it is taken. Does the philosopher really point out paths to be followed? Of course not, no more than does the scientist whose work

Dewey also describes in those same terms. Do both of them do something that is more or less akin to pointing out paths? Well, yes, I suppose they could be said to do so. Does the image better fit what the scientist does than what Dewey sees the philosopher as doing? I believe it might, though I will hold off saying why I believe that until it is time to take a final look at Dewey's use of the term *philosophic method*.

Meanwhile, let us now turn to a second set of images that Dewey draws upon when referring to his own experience as a philosopher. These show up, however, far more often in his poetry, which was not written for public consumption, than in his published writings.

DEWEY'S NAUTICAL IMAGERY

Dewey, so far as I know, was not a seasoned mariner. I have never seen a photo of him in appropriate togs aboard a boat of any kind. Nor do I know of any reference to sailing or yachting in the scant autobiographical record he left behind. This is not to say that he never participated in such activity. He certainly may have done so. But if he did, he seems to have kept it more or less a secret.

Yet he did seem drawn to nautical imagery in his poetry. References to ships and sailing in one form or another crop up in at least half a dozen of his poems. Moreover, where they do he often seems to be referring to some aspect of his own intellectual journeyings. Furthermore, the conditions described in such references are usually far from idyllic. The seafarer in Dewey's poems is very often fogbound, adrift, or otherwise at sea. In a small poem titled "Respite," for example, he complains,

> The shallow seas o'errun the sand
> Smoking fogs the deep waters hide
> A space in covert I abide
> Nor wish to sail, nor care to land.
> (1977, 26)

Another begins:

> The rope is cut, the anchor falls
> And is left alone in the mud,
> Submerged.

Conditions grow worse as the poem unfolds:

> *Oozy the slime;*
> *I can feel string sea weeds coming,*
> *Tangling, strangling. Rust eats.*
> *Sinks the anchor deeper, ever deeper,*
> *In the mud.*
> *Not an anchor now, just stuff,*
> *Part of the world's eternal waste*
> *Some used up, some unused.*
> *It presses hard. It hurts*
> *The soft bosom of the sea depths,*
> *Cruelly it presses*
> *And hurts.*
> *The yielding softness*
> *Covers and engulfs.*
> *No anchor now—*
> *Waste and oozy slime*

And the poem ends:

> *Drifts the ship. The rope end, cut,*
> *Flaps upon the side and knocks,*
> *Knocks. You can hear it through the*
> *blowing wind,*
> *And through the screeching of the sails*
> *On the masts.*
> *And when I cannot hear it I know*
> *It flaps and knocks*
> *All the time.*
> *(1977, 43–44)*

It is hard to know what to make of Dewey's poetic references to being lost at sea and drifting about without anchor in fog-shrouded waters. Perhaps it's best not to make too much of such talk. Yet it is tempting all the same to think about whether and how those images of seagoing misadventures might connect somehow to Dewey's particular way of doing philosophy. Could it be, for example, that Dewey's view of philosophy as having no subject matter of its own contributes in some measure to his feelings of being "adrift" from time to time in his philosophical journeying? Might his avowal of empiricism rob him of "navigational guidance" in some way, there being neither a "light from above" nor an ultimate goal of any kind toward which all of philosophy is headed? Is one more likely to encounter "fog" when traversing the route between practice and theory than when foregoing such a journey? In short, does a Deweyan philosopher face greater doubt and uncertainty in general than do philosophers of some other stripe—absolute idealists, let's say, or absolute realists?

I think it unwise to jump prematurely to that conclusion. For if one reads either Dewey's poems or his prose carefully, one finds as much evidence of self-confidence in what he was doing and where he was going as one finds evidence of uncertainty and doubt. In fact, I would say that, overall, the former far exceeds the latter, especially in his published work. Indeed, there are times when I almost wish the imbalance there were somewhat less in favor of a kind of buoyant self-assuredness. In his poems, I find, he often strikes a better balance, as in these brief lines, which were introduced at the start of this chapter:

> *Like formless fog on aimless cruise*
> *Over fens whence pallid waters ooze*
> *Wand'ring I drift—*
>
> *But look! Upon the leaden sky—*
> *Whereto my thoughts, aweary, scarce may fly*
> *A gleam, a rift—*
>
> *Now to a sweet and sunlit land,*
> *By heaven's own blue in peace o'erspanned,*
> *I come, swift, swift—*
> *(1977, 77–78)*

Or consider this longer verse, already presented in two parts at the start of the Introduction and Chapter 3. It is entitled "Truth's Torch," and though it does not contain nautical imagery, it does end in fog, which at least hints at the possibility of a body of water somewhere nearby.

> *Think not the torch*
> *Is one of joy and light.*
> *It's scatter'd sparks but scorch*
> *And die in falling night.*
>
> *Heed not the lies*
> *In idleness conceivèd*
> *Of truth's illumined skies*
> *For aye and aye retreivèd.*

No course is lit
By light that former burned
From darkness bit by bit
The present road is learned.

Tho space shines bright
And paths are trodden clear
Never to thy searching sight
Does the true road appear

Till dart th'arrows
Of thine own lifted flame
Through clinging fogs that close
And hide the journey's aim.
(1977, 64–65)

The suggestion of the poem seems to be that the traveler can depend only on himself to light the way but that his sole means of illumination, his "own lifted flame," is not very powerful and does not penetrate the foggy darkness very far. It clearly is not powerful enough to reveal "the journey's aim." Moreover, no other source of illumination will do any better. Neither "light that former burned" nor the idly conceived notion that someday truth itself will illumine the skies once and for all can be relied upon. Each traveler carries his own flame.

Does the poem imply that the journey really has no aim? It leaves that an open question. Yet I believe Dewey's own view to be that the traveler continually establishes and reestablishes his own aim or aims as he goes along. He does so, moreover, constrained by the conditions that his high-held flame partially illumines and the clinging fog partially enshrouds. Certainty and uncertainty coexist every step of the way.

CHAPTER 5

Philosophic Method Reconsidered

I believe that the method of empirical naturalism presented in this volume provides the way, and the only way . . . by which one can freely accept the standpoint and conclusions of modern science: the way by which we can be genuinely naturalistic and yet maintain cherished values, provided they are critically clarified and reinforced.
—*John Dewey, Experience and Nature*, LW1, 4

Dewey assumes that science shows what intelligence is and that what intelligent practice is pretty much follows from that; the mission of philosophy is to get the Enlightenment to happen.
—*Stanley Cavell, This New Yet Unapproachable America*, 1989, 95

The history of thought sufficiently manifests the need for a method of procedure that sets pointing, finding and showing, ahead of methods that substitute ratiocination and its conclusions for things that are done, suffered and imagined.
—*John Dewey, Experience and Nature*, LW1, 373

Dewey tried to dismantle the history of philosophy by not attending to it. . . . Dewey was debunking rather than replacing philosophy, and in a way this was part of a great journalistic tradition in America—the tradition of the muckraker.
—Stanley Cavell, in Giovanna Borradori,
The American Philosopher, 1994, 124

The first chapter of *Experience and Nature* in both of its published versions was, as we know, entitled "Experience and Philosophic Method." I now want to take a renewed look at the second of those two terms in light of some of the things that were said in the previous chapter about Dewey's use of figurative language. Crudely expressed, the question I want to explore in this chapter has to do with how seriously, which is to say how literally, we are to take the term *philosophic method*. To make that question somewhat less crude and therefore more amenable to inquiry I have divided it into four subquestions, a couple of them with alternate wordings. These are:

1. Is Dewey's philosophic method truly a *method*? Or, less rhetorically, in what sense might that term apply?
2. How does Dewey's philosophic method relate to what is commonly called *the scientific method*?
3. Is Dewey's philosophic method the only one there is?
4. Is Dewey's use of the term *philosophic method* potentially misleading? Might it inadvertently contribute to a false picture of the philosopher's task?

I will take up each of these questions in turn.

1. IS DEWEY'S TRULY A METHOD?

Is Dewey's philosophic method truly a method? Or, less rhetorically, in what sense might the latter term apply? What makes a way of doing something a method? How is the term defined? The *Oxford English Dictionary* offers two broad definitions: an ancient (Greek) one and a more modern (Latin) one. The definition derived from the Greeks applies the term *method* to any mode of investigation, any procedure for attaining an objective. The Latin usage, developed by logicians of the sixteenth century, refers to a systematic or orderly arrangement of thoughts and topics for investigation.

The distinction between them is not sharp and clean, but the two etymologies give backing to the notion that there is a weak and a strong sense of the term. In the weak sense, a *method* is just any way at all of getting something done, as in an advertised method of painless tooth extraction, let's say; in the strong sense, it is an explicitly defined way of achieving that or any other goal. Examples of the latter, ranging across all manner of doing, might include the steps to follow in developing a mathematical proof, the printed directions for assembling a mechanical object, the recipe for preparing a particular dish, and so on. Compared with such highly specified routines, *philosophic method*, as Dewey uses the term, falls decidedly on the weak side.

Yet to observe that Dewey uses the term *method* in its weak sense is not to imply that what he calls *philosophic method* totally lacks system or order. He does, after all, offer suggestions about where to begin one's philosophic inquiry and where to end it. More than that, he lays out a procedure sequentially. He talks about where to start (i.e., with ordinary experience), what to do next (i.e., reflect, theorize on the situation from an abstract perspective), what to do after that (i.e., return to the initial set of conditions to test one's proposed solution), and what to do once the complete sequence has been enacted (i.e., if it works, fine; if not, go back to theorizing and keep testing until one hits upon a better idea).

This is only to say that if one should pause at any one of those steps to ask for greater detail about how to proceed, a fuller answer is most unlikely. Therefore, the answer to the initial question framed at the start has to be no. Dewey's philosophic method is a *method* only in a weak sense.

2. WHAT IS THE RELATION TO THE SCIENTIFIC METHOD?

How does Dewey's philosophic method relate to what is commonly called the scientific method? The relationship between Dewey's philosophic thought and the enterprise of science constitutes a bit of a puzzle. On the one hand, he pays a fair amount of attention to science and the scientific method in a number of his writings. Moreover, he does so admiringly most of the time. He lauds the many accomplishments of science. He also obviously believes that its practitioners have much to teach everyone about the conduct of inquiry. Philosophers in particular, it seems, would be well-advised to become more scientific in their approach in certain respects than Dewey found them to be in his day.

On the other hand, Dewey also expresses misgivings about developing too close a relationship between science and philosophy. He is chary, as we have seen, about having philosophers begin their investigations within the provinces of science. He fears that they may become so used to working within that kind of specialized and purified environment, with its refined tools and problems, that they cease to be interested in turning their professional attention to the messier affairs of ordinary life. He also worries about their treating the latest scientific findings as absolute knowledge rather than as provisional outlooks.

These countervailing points of view toward science make it hard to know what to make of Dewey's call for a closer rapprochement between philosophy and science in general and for a more scientific approach to philosophical investigation. Just how close a resemblance does he envision developing between the two modes of investigation? Is he calling upon philosophers to emulate scientists in their eschewal of subjectivity and their utter devotion to objectivity? Not at all, I would say. In fact, he objects to the overuse of that distinction, as we have already seen. Does he want to make science the supreme arbiter in matters of philosophic method? Again, I would say not at all. Yet his advocacy of a closer relationship between philosophy and science has been read in those extreme terms by more than one critic.[1]

Stanley Cavell, who is known to be a very careful and generous reader of both literary and philosophical texts, once gave voice to that line of criticism in an essay that concentrated chiefly on Emerson's well-known essay "Experience." As I quoted at the beginning of this chapter, Cavell wrote,

> For Emerson, as for Kant, putting the philosophical intellect into practice remains a question for philosophy. For a thinker such as John Dewey it becomes, as I might put it, merely a problem. That is, Dewey assumes that science shows what intelligence is and that what intelligent practice is pretty much follows from that; the mission of philosophy is to get the Enlightenment to happen. (1979, 95)

But Cavell has to be wrong in that judgment. Dewey's view of philosophy's mission can hardly be reduced to the slogan: "Get the Enlightenment to happen!" He was, if anything, a harsh critic of many of the central figures of the British and French Enlightenment. Indeed, if we look closely at what it is about science that Dewey most admires, it is less that science *enlightens* than that it *emancipates*, less that it yields knowledge than that it offers the promise of freedom. Freedom from what? From superstition, from stultifying tradition, from despotic authority. How does it do so? Chiefly through science-as-method, rather than science-as-knowledge. Dewey explains,

> We discover that we believe many things not because the things are so, but because we have become habituated through the weight of authority, by imitation, prestige, instruction, the unconscious effect of language, etc. We learn, in short, that qualities which we attribute to objects ought to be imputed to our own ways of experiencing them, and that these in turn are due to the force of intercourse and custom. This discovery marks an emancipation; it purifies and remakes the objects of our direct or primary experience (LW1, 14).

As to Cavell's additional claim that "Dewey assumes that science shows what intelligence is and that what intelligent practice is pretty much follows from that," my own reading of Dewey leaves me with a very different impression. As I read what he says about science, it does not show what intelligence *is* so much as it shows what intelligence *takes*. And what is that? What does a masterful exercise of intelligence, which, Dewey would remind us, is shorthand for *intelligently guided experience*, actually take?

To begin, it takes a host of personal dispositions, habits, and attitudes—among them patience, persistence, open-mindedness, careful observation, unflagging attention to detail, reflection, experimentation, imagination, an abiding faith in one's own capacity to pursue the truth, an enduring delight in that pursuit, and even—all cautious proprieties aside—a undying love of it. It also takes a public—a community of founders and forebears, collaborators and critics, well-wishers and beneficiaries. It takes a language, plus the capacity to put that language to work.

Does the masterful exercise of intelligence by philosophers take any less than that? Surely not, though it may call for a somewhat different alignment of many of those same components. It may also require strengths and capabilities beyond those named; the capacity to listen carefully to what others say and write, paying particular attention to subtle nuances of meaning, may be of far greater importance to philosophers than to physical scientists. So too the former's ability to speak and write in response to what they hear and read. It may also be that philosophers require a different kind of physical and social setting in which to exercise their intelligence. Perhaps they need a different kind of public as well.

Dewey understood those differences. He respected them. He never sought to erase the distinction between science and philosophy. Nor did he ever suggest that the two endeavors should be pursued identically. As has been said, he did, however, believe that science had something to teach everyone (philosophers included) about the conduct of inquiry. What it taught was not formulaic. It was not a lesson about doing this and then doing that. It was, instead, a lesson of reverence and faith, though one attuned to the limits and potentialities of the world as experienced. Its reverence (Dewey called it "piety") arose in response to the fullness and the richness of human experience; its faith resided in the self-correcting capacity of experience when under the guidance of a dedicated investigator.[2]

The term *scientific method* has been around for so long and is held in such esteem that it seems almost an affront to common sense (and a slur to science itself) to suggest that there may be no such thing in a literal sense. Yet that is what I am suggesting. This is not to say that scientists lack criteria for deciding when one of their fellow scientists has stepped out of line or failed to follow standard procedures or violated an agreed-upon code of ethics. Nor does it deny the crucial significance of particular skills or techniques for getting specific scientific jobs done—staining a slide specimen, tracking a star in an observatory, splicing genes, and so forth. All I am questioning is whether that complicated collection of attitudes, expectations, standards, skills, and what have you add up to anything that is readily identifiable as *the*, or even *a*, scientific method. Instead of being called a *method*, what such a *potpourri* of expectations might better be called—if it has to be named—is a *practice*, a *tradition*, or even a *way of life*.

If that state of affairs applies to the use of the term *scientific method*, it does so even more emphatically, I would say, to *philosophic method*. For with respect to the latter, as against the former, there are even fewer agreed-upon standards, codes, and techniques to give substance to the notion of method in the strong sense of the term. Philosophers, like scientists, do join communities of fellow practitioners with whom they have much in common. Yet even within those communities not everyone sees eye to eye about how to proceed. They may agree vaguely on some points, but certainly not enough to allow them to move along in a manner that could be properly called *methodical*.

3. WHAT OF OTHER PHILOSOPHIC METHODS?

Is Dewey's philosophic method the only one there is? Obviously not, though Dewey sometimes speaks as though it were the only one, or at least that is how his words are taken by some. Yet we know that innumerable philosophers before Dewey made use of some kind of method (at least in the weak sense) without its being of the kind that Dewey later advocated. Similarly, vast numbers of philosophers during Dewey's own time and since have failed to follow his methodological advice. Why, then, even raise the question?

I do so as a way of addressing an aspect of Dewey's way of working that he does not himself address, yet it is one that others have noted and remarked upon. For an apt example, I again draw upon a casual remark of Stanley Cavell's (partially quoted earlier). Speaking to an interviewer, Cavell once charged Dewey with having "tried to dismantle the history of philosophy by not attending to it" (Borradori, 1994, 124). He continued,

> In a sense, not attending to it is also a way of doing a kind of social good. Dewey was debunking rather than replacing philosophy, and in a way this was part of a great journalistic tradition in America—the tradition of the muckraker. Instead of finding that philosophy comes from the deepest of spiritual needs, which conflict with themselves, you find that it has its origin in social muck (pp. 124–125).

Once again I find myself disagreeing with Cavell's evaluation of Dewey, even though I can begin to understand how he may have come to his harsh judgment. Dewey was indeed critical and at times sharply dismissive of some of the philosophic positions with which he disagreed. In previous chapters we have encountered ample evidence of such an attitude. Was he often too dismissive? To my way of thinking, he often was. I further believe he would have said so himself if queried. In fact, he did say so, as we saw in chapter 4.

Yet Dewey was by no means out to debunk philosophy in general. He was himself a philosopher through and through and remained so throughout his life. With due respect to Cavell, I hold that he *was* seeking to replace philosophy with philosophy—the philosophy of his opponents with that of his own. Were his efforts to do so journalistic in manner? Was his style of criticism in the great American tradition of the muckraker? I fail to see how.

He was himself aware of the deficiencies of his way of writing. Yet he did not look upon that as a grave hindrance in getting his message across. As he once confessed to a friend, "I'm deeply aware of my lack of art in writing. But in the main I think I am headed right and it will all come out in the wash that needs to." He added, "It [my writing] is too balanced in thought to have a grip on the reader, or to have its meaning very perceptible. But when it gets a man it sticks—so much may be said" (reported in Rockefeller, 1991, 332–33).

On several occasions he deigns to point out that the social conditions of Ancient Greece—the presence there of slavery, for example—may have had something to do with the low esteem accorded manual labor and thus with the drawing of a sharp distinction between theory and practice. Generalizations of that order (and Dewey was fond of making such sweeping statements) may be controversial, but I would hardly call them *muckraking* in either tone or intent.

What of Cavell's notion that philosophy arises from the deepest of spiritual needs? Was Dewey oblivious to philosophy's origins in that sense? Not at all—indeed, I think quite the opposite. In the interview from which the above quotation was taken, Cavell went on to observe that the only way out of the conflict created by such opposing spiritual needs is through their mutual negation, which "is itself a kind of spiritual torture." "In Dewey," he complained, "you don't have spiritual torture" (Borradori, 1994, 125).

I am not sure what kind of spiritual torture Cavell had in mind when he made that statement, but I would be quick to agree that Dewey does not come across as a tortured soul in any of his writings that I can think of, leaving aside, of course, the muffled *cris du coeur* that sound so repeatedly and so poignantly in his poetry. In the one autobiographical statement to which I have already made reference (LW5, 10), he does speak of experiencing some of the prominent dualisms of his youth as a kind of "inward laceration," but I suspect that such feelings would fall short of Cavell's tacit criterion.

Yet, unless I am very wrong, what I have referred to throughout this book as Dewey's avowed empiricism gives voice to an enduring spiritual need on his part, an emotional craving far more powerful, I now believe, than I had realized at the start of my investigation. Its goal: the discovery of a way of doing philosophy that is shorn of intellectual pretensions and other-worldly ambitions, a philosophy of the *agora* as much as of the *academy,* one capable of addressing the issues of the day yet sufficiently reflective in its operation to call for the exercise of Dewey's special talent for ascending the ladder of abstraction and gazing on the scene below from a lofty perch.

Returning to the question of why Dewey made it sound as though only one philosophic method existed, I suspect the answer might have something to do with Dewey's struggle to overcome his own intellectual history.

For Dewey, the crucial and irreversible move within modern philosophy was its turning away from absolute idealism and its ultimate embrace of empiricism (which he sometimes called "experimentalism"). That transformation was one that he himself had undergone as a young adult, beginning in his days as a graduate student at Johns Hopkins University and culminating during the early years of his academic career.[3]

The move was decisive for Dewey in a number of ways. More-over, it had both positive and negative consequences. On the positive side, it brought his philosophic thinking into closer alignment with developments taking place within the physical and natural sciences (with Darwinian thought in particular). On the negative side, it defined his opposition. In his day-to-day affiliations, it separated him definitively from all who clung to supernaturalism in any of its varied forms. It was also an ostracizing move professionally in two different ways.

It not only drove a wedge between Dewey and those philosophers who persisted in chasing after the impossible dream of absolute idealism;[4] it also led to his ultimate estrangement from those who shared his aversion to such otherworldly pursuits but who at the same time chose to put philosophy on a firmer footing intellectually through the rigorous application of symbolic logic and other forms of quasi-mathematical reasoning.[5] The latter as well as the former, in Dewey's view, were pursuing chimera. Figuratively speaking, the realists dreamed of exiting experience through its basement door. They sought its mooring in physical reality. The idealists dreamed of exiting through its skylight. They sought to soar beyond experience into the ether of the spiritual.[6] Both dreams, of course, are as totally fanciful as the picture I have just used to convey the difference between them.

Dewey's embrace of (I would prefer saying "conversion to") wholehearted empiricism succeeded in effecting a synthesis (how stable or unstable is a question yet to be considered) of his developing philosophic interests and his awakening social consciousness. That synthesis did not only allow him to turn from matters that occupied the attention of many of his most highly esteemed fellow philosophers at universities at home and abroad but virtually demanded that he do so. His founding of the Laboratory School at the University of Chicago in 1897 was the quintessential expression of that demand.[7]

The chief conclusion that I derive from that perspective on Dewey's intellectual coming-of-age is that he wound up being as firmly *opposed* to those views that ran counter to his own convictions as he was *for* the view that he himself espoused. By the time he had begun to write *Experience and Nature*—and even long before then—he had become not only an avowed empiricist but also a rank enemy of non-empiricists. Indeed, I now see him as having been stauncher in his opposition to nonempiricism than he was in his enthusiasm for his own position.

This is not the easiest of conclusions to defend, I must admit, for as a public figure Dewey was looked upon as a kind and gentle person, one whose enthusiasms far outshone his antipathies.[8] The public in general remembers him as a champion of democracy, a forward-looking educational crusader, and an advocate of social harmony. He is remembered in those terms far more readily than as a strident and sharp-tongued critic of those with whom he disagreed. His style of argument was typically low-keyed and even-tempered. Even his enemies seldom felt his sting.

Yet Dewey did harbor strong feelings about a lot of things. This becomes evident if we read almost any of his major works with care. The slow and measured pace of his prose belies its emotional depth. The latter often takes repeated reading to discern.

One of the things that he felt most strongly about (nowhere more clearly evinced than in *Experience and Nature*) was the tendency among philosophers (from the Greeks forward) to turn their backs on human experience, to make light of its importance, even to imagine themselves capable of transcending its constraints. The culmination of that tendency gave rise to the various forms of nonempiricism that Dewey so vehemently opposed throughout most of his career. It was nonempiricism in one or another of its guises that invariably violated Dewey's fundamental principle of continuity.[9] It did so by positing a *dis*continuity of one kind or another between experience and something else—nature, reality, spirit, world, call it what you will—a discontinuity that philosophy itself (the form of philosophy to which Dewey was opposed) aspired to breach through thought alone.

Why was Dewey's opposition to the nonempiricists so covertly vehement? It was so, I believe, because he had once been among their number. He had managed to overcome within himself the same tendency he later so adamantly opposed in others. Moreover, if my guess is right, he continued to feel the lure of that way of thinking. He felt its strong tug throughout his life. As he later experienced it, it was not exactly a tug in the direction of trying to *escape* experience. Rather, it pulled him away from experience's more enveloping entanglements.

Perhaps that impulse to escape the complexity of the everyday world is sufficiently widespread among philosophers to be thought of as *the* philosophical urge. Whatever may be the case, the tug for Dewey, if my guess is right, was more than sheerly intellectual. It was also a matter of both temperament and cultural conditioning. My sense is that Dewey's personal struggle with that inclination strengthened his opposition to the nonempiricists.

He implies as much in the one essay that I know of in which he explicitly discusses his development as a philosopher, a portion of which I have already quoted. The essay appeared in 1930, shortly after publication of the revised edition of *Experience and Nature*. He there reports,

> I imagine that my development has been controlled largely by a struggle between a native inclination toward the schematic and formally logical, and those incidents of personal experience that compelled me to take account of actual material (LW5, 150).

What Dewey meant by "a native inclination toward the schematic and formally logical" was, I believe, a penchant for trafficking in the kind of truths that required no empirical foraging about, truths that were reached by a combination of reason and common sense. He was by nature far more of a thinker than a doer, even though he was in his day widely esteemed for his active involvement in a wide range of social affairs. As he reported at the celebration honoring his seventieth birthday,

> One of the conditions of happiness is the opportunity of a calling, a career which somehow is congenial to one's own temperament. And I have had the sheer luck or fortune to be engaged in the occupation of thinking; and while I am quite regular at my meals I think that I may say that I had rather work—and perhaps even more play—with ideas and thinking than eat (LW5, 420).

He also preferred writing about general truths to becoming immersed in more timely matters. Yet, again, he was well known in his day as an astute social commentator. He ascribes the latter kind of involvement to the psychological dynamics of overcompensation. He explains,

> Probably there is in the consciously articulated ideas of every thinker an overweighting of just those things that are contrary to his natural tendencies, an emphasis upon those things that are contrary to his intrinsic bent, and with which, therefore, he has to struggle to bring to expression, while

the native bent, on the other hand, can take care of itself. Anyway a case might be made out for the proposition that the emphasis upon the concrete, empirical, and "practical" in my later writings is partly due to considerations of this nature. It was a reaction against what was more natural, and it served as a protest and protection against something in myself which, in the pressure of the weight of actual experiences, I knew to be a weakness (LW5, 151).

He further intimates that some of the things he said against those with whom he disagreed were in truth a form of self-criticism.

It is, I suppose, becoming a commonplace that when anyone is unduly concerned with controversy, the remarks that seem to be directed against others are really concerned with a struggle that is going on inside himself (LW5, 151).

What Dewey says next about that internal struggle brings us close to the core of his concern over philosophic method. He begins with a revealing insight about his experience as a writer.

During the time when the schematic interest predominated, writing was comparatively easy; there were even compliments upon the clearness of my style. Since then thinking and writing have been hard work (LW5, 151).

What made thinking and writing so hard, Dewey explains as follows:

It is easy to give way to the dialectical development of a theme; the pressure of concrete experiences was, however, sufficiently heavy, so that a sense of intellectual honesty prevented a surrender to that course. But, on the other hand, the formal interest persisted (LW5, 151).

It is what happened as a consequence of that struggle between the press of concrete experience on the one hand and the persistence of Dewey's interest in the formal and the logical on the other that brings us to the heart of what Dewey was seeking. The consequence, as he described it, was

an inner demand for an intellectual technique that would be consistent and yet capable of flexible adaptation to the concrete diversity of experienced things (LW5, 151).

He concludes with an acknowledgment of his own hypersensitivity to the "specious lucidity and simplicity" of other thinkers and writers who managed to display such false virtues "by the mere process of ignoring considerations which a greater respect for concrete materials of experience would have forced upon them" (LW5, 151).

Dewey's overall response to those philosophers, past and present, who seemingly lack respect for, and thereby ignore, the concrete materials of experience is simply to ignore them more or less, which doubtless contributes to the impression, as voiced in Cavell's complaint, that Dewey turns his back on philosophy. He does, of course, believe that his own philosophic method is the only one that explicitly acknowledges both the necessity and the inevitability of coming to grips with those concrete materials of experience. This is why he calls it, among other things, the only method by which one can freely accept the standpoint and conclusions of modern science. In turning his back on the past and on the activities of many of his contemporaries, he does not, however, resign from the club. He remains an insider throughout his life, though one bent on reform and privately disgruntled from time to time with the way things were going. With due respect to Cavell, I argue that Dewey was not trying to dismantle the history of philosophy by not attending to it. He chose not to attend to much of that history, I would prefer to say, because doing so did not seem to him to serve any worthwhile purpose. It promised to be of little help in advancing his program of reforming philosophy.

Might he have been mistaken on that score? Might he have strengthened his hand among his fellow philosophers, then and now, if he had wrestled more energetically and more publicly with the positions taken by his adversaries, living and dead? Cavell's criticism implies an affirmative answer to that question. I am not sure how to answer it. There are times when I would like to know in much more detail than he provides precisely what he saw wrong with this or that idea borrowed from the Greeks or with the details of Kant's deontology or Hegel's dialectic. Likewise, I often would like to have seen him engage the logical positivists more directly or respond more fully to Russell's criticism of his position. He chose instead to avoid such contentious engagements in the main and to spend most of his time as an author enacting the philosophical program outlined in the introductory material to *Experience and Nature* and elsewhere. Was that an unfortunate choice? As much as I would have relished from time to time more writings of the type just described, I cannot bring myself to fault him for choosing as he did.

4. IS DEWEY'S USAGE MISLEADING?

Is Dewey's use of the term "philosophic method" potentially misleading? Might it inadvertently contribute to a false picture of the philosopher's task? The preceding two questions are meant to sound rhetorical. An affirmative answer to each of them is implied. There is, it seems to me, something potentially misleading about Dewey's use of the term *philosophic method*. Furthermore, it is not just that the word *method* is likely to be taken in its strong rather than its weak sense, which I cautioned against earlier, though taking it in that sense certainly adds to the problem.

The term is misleading additionally, however, in that the stress Dewey places upon it focuses attention on the philosopher's actual moves—on what steps and in what sequence he or she is to take them—and thus diverts attention from a broader conception of the philosopher's task. This broader conception would take into account such matters as the philosopher's social and moral commitments, among other things, matters that were of great moment to Dewey, as we have seen.

Dewey was fond of the word *method*. He called his way of working "the method of empirical naturalism." He also spoke of it comparatively as "a method of procedure that set pointing, finding, and showing, ahead of methods that substitute ratiocination and its conclusions for things that are done, suffered and imagined" (LW1, 373). But as the word is used in those and other of his descriptions, it cloaks as much as it reveals.

What stands out more than anything when one reflects on Dewey's philosophic position is the range and breadth of the issues calling for philosophical analysis. Thus if we look closely at his emphasis on the so-called denotative method, for example, what we find is not simply that it calls upon philosophers to point at features of the world in a manner akin to that of all other avowed empiricists. Of far greater importance is the question of what they are invited to point *at*. What, in short, according to Dewey, are philosophers to take as their subject matter?

Dewey has more than one answer to that question, although he prefers one over most others. His favorite seems to be that philosophy has no subject matter of its own. Philosophers are free to explore all of experience, examining one form of it after the other, as personal proclivities and local circumstances allow. This is the answer he presents in the original first chapter of *Experience and Nature*, readers will recall.

Another answer, which he begins to formulate in the longer of the two unfinished re-introductions to *Experience and Nature*, is that the "standing problem" for Western philosophy throughout its entire history has been and continues to be "the connection-and-distinction of what on one side is regarded as *human* and on the other side as *natural*" (LW1, 331). This answer leaves open the question of whether other problems beyond the aforementioned "standing problem" exist for philosophers to investigate, but it certainly establishes the latter as having priority over any others.

Yet a third answer to the question of philosophy's subject matter begins with a contrast between two ostensible starting places for philosophical investigations. It seemingly offers a choice between them, but the gesture turns out to be rhetorical. Dewey asks: "Shall philosophy set out from and with the macroscopic or with the microscopic; with the gross and complex or with the minute and elemental?" (LW5, 174).

His answer, as one might guess, is to start with the macroscopic. He explains what that means:

> Social phenomena constitute what I mean by the macroscopic. They are the large, the largest, most inclusive and most complex of all the phenomena with which mind has to deal. They also present the problems with which thought occupies itself in their most direct, urgent and practical form (LW5, 175).

The only other option, as he goes on to say, is to begin with "the results of special analyses, mathematical, physical and biological" (LW5, 175). That, of course, is where those philosophers whom Dewey calls "the rationalists" had been starting their investigations for centuries. Many continued to do so in Dewey's own day.

The problem with starting out with the results of a special analysis of some kind, rather than with unanalyzed, gross phenomena, is that the practice too easily leads to "the conversion of a temporary abstraction from the complex gross scene into a permanent and fixed isolation" (LW5, 176). Dewey looks upon that conversion as being "the ultimate source of all philosophic fallacies and errors" (LW5, 176). In fact, he typically refers to it as *the* philosophical fallacy.

Now the point about all three of these answers to the question of what philosophy is to study is that Dewey makes them out to be essentially methodological in nature. With respect to the third answer, for example, he says that what is involved is "the ultimate basis and nature of philosophic method" (LW5, 174). He treats the other two in similar fashion. But is *method* the sole or even the best way of characterizing all that is involved in any of those answers? I tend to think not.

The trouble with Dewey's use (or as I see it, his overuse) of the term *philosophic method* is that it flirts with the same fallacy that he accuses the rationalists of committing. It takes "a temporary abstraction from the complex gross scene" (LW5, 176), which is to say, one particular aspect of that complex form of experience that goes by the name of philosophy, and converts it into something like "a permanent and fixed isolation" (LW5, 176). It highlights philosophy's "moves" (as Dewey would like to see them made) at the expense of every other way of conceptualizing all that it takes to play philosophy's game, if I may employ the Wittgensteinian notion of *game* without slighting philosophy's intellectual status in any way.

This is not to say that such moves are unimportant and should not be highlighted. On the contrary, they fully deserve the kind of attention that Dewey gives them. The problem is that the way he employs the rubric *philosophic method* as an umbrella term makes it appear that the "doing" of philosophy is a matter of making such moves and little else. Dewey knows better than that, of course, but his repeated use of the term tends to overshadow that knowledge.

What does it take beyond making moves to play philosophy's game as Dewey would like to see it played? It takes a lot more, as a close look at Dewey's own performance as a philosopher readily reveals. It takes a certain perspective on experience and on human affairs in general. As we have just seen, Dewey calls that perspective "macroscopic" in at least one of its portrayals. Figuratively, it could as easily be called a bird's-eye view or a view from afar, the sort of outlook that befits a mapmaker. Yet there are certain things that such a view could not be called, as we have also seen. It could not be called a God's-eye view, a Platonic perspective, or even, perhaps, a view from Mars. Dewey's outlook is fundamentally and irrevocably humanistic in orientation.

It additionally takes a kind of receptivity to things as they are and to conditions as they exist, a worldliness, one might say. Yet that willingness to look unflinchingly at current conditions is combined in Dewey's pragmatic outlook with a firm conviction that many of those conditions can be better than they are. A corollary conviction is that such improvements can come about only through human effort. The latter is almost an article of faith for Dewey. Yet it is not a blind faith. Like knowledge itself, it rests on experience.

The doing of philosophy is volitional. It is a matter of choice. It involves wanting to play philosophy's game. That wanting to play rests in part on the rewards of playing—on the intrinsic pleasures that philosophy gives its practitioners—and in part on a conception of the good it might do for others. Dewey, as we have seen, found philosophy to be rewarding as a way of life for himself, and he also believed in its potential benefits to the society at large.

Philosophy calls upon its practitioners to adopt a set of attitudes that allow for the exercise of reflective thought. These include a certain tolerance of ambiguity, a respect for the opinions of others, an open-mindedness with respect to contrary views, a patience in following the intricacies of a complex argument, and so forth. Those same attitudes in combination serve other practitioners as well, naturally enough, making it unwise to think of them as being uniquely philosophic in nature. Yet they are so crucial to an adequate performance of the philosopher's task that an acknowledgment of their centrality almost has to be a part of any far-reaching discussion of that topic.

Philosophy requires language, a way of speaking and writing that not only articulates the philosopher's own views but does so in a manner that is recognized by others as being philosophic in form as much as in content. Dewey acknowledged that requirement in the autobiographical essay to which I have already referred. He there discussed how easy it was to write philosophical treatises that dealt with questions systematically and logically and how much more difficult writing became when he decided that philosophy had to take into account empirical states of affairs. A new kind of writing was called for, owing to a shift in the philosophy's task.

As this brief overview is intended to reveal, what it takes to play philosophy's game involves much more than method alone. It also involves a complex assortment of intentions, beliefs, attitudes, values, skills, points of view, modes of language, and much more. Or at least its requirements can be helpfully looked upon in those various ways. For the point of the above is not that the "doing" of philosophy is somehow *made up* of a combination of beliefs, attitudes, and so forth, much like the ingredients of an Irish stew. Rather, it is that such terms (and others like them) provide alternate ways of conceptualizing various aspects of the whole (the "gross phenomenon") of living the philosophic life as Dewey recommends. As I have tried to make clear in this book, all of those ways of looking at philosophy are either tacitly or explicitly expressed in his repeated attempts to introduce and re-introduce *Experience and Nature* to its continuing audience of readers.

Afterword

When man is drawing into what withdraws, he points into what withdraws. As we are drawing that way we are a sign, a pointer. But we are pointing then at something which has not, not yet, been transposed into the language of our speech. We are a sign that is not read.
—Martin Heidegger, *What is Called Thinking?*, 1968, 18

This frail ship I load with limitless freight
Of hopes and loves. Turning to think upon
The pathless unruled waters, waste and wan
Where she must adventure, or soon or late,
Past winds that gnaw and seas that ne'er abate,
To find a port far beyond all that's yon,
Where not even stauncher barks have gone—
I shudder, half afraid and half elate.
—*Poems of John Dewey*, 1977, 27

Anyone who searches the great thinkers for their opinions and viewpoints can be sure of going astray before obtaining a result, i.e. the formula or signpost for a philosophy.
—Martin Heidegger, *An Introduction to Metaphysics*, 1987, 115

This book began as an attempt to discover where Dewey was heading philosophically—the direction in which his work was pointing, as Heidegger might say—during the later portion of his life. I had read, some time back, Heidegger's remark that the searcher after truth is a sign that is not read, but I had not come upon his subsequent warning about undertaking such a search until it was too late. I was nearly finished with the bulk of my writing when I ran across it in his *Introduction to Metaphysics*. But it would not have made much difference anyway, I must say. For I was not out to find a signpost or a formula for a

95

philosophy. At least that was not the way I would have phrased my ambition at the start. My goal was much more modest than that. I was simply trying to figure out why Dewey seemed to be having such a hard time introducing *Experience and Nature* to its various audiences as the book was revised and prepared for reissuance over the years.

My hunch was that his apparent difficulty (which is how I initially conceived of what he must have been experiencing) may have reflected some discomfort with his own view of philosophy. Having spent a reasonable amount of time trying to understand that view, I was naturally curious about any change that he might have been trying to effect toward the close of his career.

I did indeed find evidence of the change that I had vaguely surmised might be there, although I am not sure that *change* is the right word to describe it. It was more like a barely discernible shift in direction, a slow drift from one compass setting to another, one might say, bearing in mind Dewey's use of the word *drift* in describing the course of his labors to his friend Sidney Hook (see the epigram introducing Chapter 4). In fact, the drift seemed to me to be in two directions at once, although I can easily imagine their being combined to form a single trajectory, the way we speak of the angling wind as coming from the southwest or the northeast.

One shift of direction, if my own readings are correct, lay along the axis separating the physical sciences and the humanities. Over time, it seems to me, Dewey was gradually moving his own philosophical allegiance closer to the goals and purposes of the humanities and correspondingly further from those associated with the sciences. This is not to say that Dewey can ever be seen as turning against the sciences. Far from it. Nor does it deny his continued admiration for certain aspects of the so-called scientific method—its emphasis on experimentation and the continual testing of its theories, for example. But it is to suggest a decided tilting away from the more materialistically inclined variants of philosophical empiricism, such as those adopted by the so-called logical positivists, coupled with a correspondingly closer alignment with some of the more humanistically inclined disciplines, such as history and anthropology.

This movement in the direction of the humanities is most clearly evinced in Dewey's initial acceptance (in the original Chapter 1 of *Experience and Nature*) and subsequent disregard (in the revised version of that chapter) of those philosophers who chose to work more or less exclusively within the framework of the sciences. He later offers sharp criticism of that option. The same shift of direction is further evident in his extensive use of historical examples (particularly in the first unfinished revised Introduction), in the many references to anthropological studies, and in the proposed substitution of the word *culture* for *experience* in the book's title (in the second unfinished Re-introduction). These modifications fit together, it seems to me, to form a single directional shift.

The second drift that I discern in Dewey's four attempts to introduce *Experience and Nature* I would characterize as a pulling in of philosophy's horns. Instead of looking upon the apparent separation of experience and nature as a universal problem, which he seemed to do at the start, he comes to see it (in preparing the introduction for the book's reissuance) as being of special significance within *Western* society and as having been so for the past several centuries. He calls it our society's "standing problem," clearly implying that it may not be a standing problem worldwide, nor need it have been so throughout Western history.

This apparent contraction of philosophy's domain is in keeping with Dewey's move in the direction of the humanities, though the two changes, it seems to me, are sufficiently distinct to deserve separate mention. It is also consonant with Dewey's avowed empiricism, for which he actually proposes the label *naturalistic humanism* in his revised first chapter of 1929.

By narrowing his focus to what has become the standing problem of Western society—the specious (as he saw it) separation between experience and nature—Dewey in the late forties distances himself even further than he had earlier from the sciencelike pursuit of principles and generalizations that are purportedly timeless and culture-free. In the lengthy Re-introduction that he laid aside unfinished in 1949 he verges on openly acknowledging that even his highly vaulted "ordinary experience"—philosophy's starting place, as he would have it—has to be looked upon as culturally conditioned in a very deep sense. Therefore it is not nearly as ordinary—that is, as universal—as his formulations of the early twenties would seem to imply.

So much, then, for the two changes of direction that I find evident in the four documents that have served as the primary focus of this book. As I come to the end of this exploration, what do I now make of them? Has their revelation repaid the effort of their unveiling?

I would say it has for me personally, though not as much as I had initially hoped. Part of the reason for that has to do with my unwillingness to put too much stock in what I have found. Why? Because it comes too close to what I wanted to find. I belatedly must admit that from the start I covertly hoped to find Dewey edging away from the goals and ambitions of the hard sciences, although I may not have said so in so many words, even to myself. I wanted to see him become a less likely target for the taunts of those—like Stanley Cavell (see Chapter 5)—who were quick to dismiss him as being too enamored of the methods of science. I did not feel as strongly about seeing him openly affiliate with the more humanistically oriented disciplines, but I must say that I was not at all displeased to come upon extensive quotations from a leading historian and a well-known anthropologist in his final two forays at re-introducing *Experience and Nature*. To me he seemed perfectly at home in such company, far more so than when reporting the results of scientific experiments, which he also did from time to time. His final concentration on "the standing problem" of Western society and his proposed substitution of the term *culture* for the term *experience* in the title of his book also struck me as fitting changes, quite in keeping with my own image of him as a socially committed philosopher.

So both of the so-called drifts that I have identified are ones that I silently applauded as I came upon them. I even wished for one of them ahead of time. This, then, is the chief reason for my feeling a bit uncomfortable about the trustworthiness of my findings. I remain confident, however, that I did not just make up those changes out of whole cloth. The evidence for them may be somewhat tainted by my personal bias, but it is evidence all the same. In a guarded sense, therefore, I stand behind those two claims.

Fortunately, the evidence of change that I went looking for was not all that I found out about Dewey in the course of my investigation. I also came to look upon him personally in a different light. I came to see him as less confident about his own philosophic method than I had previously taken him to be. In fact, as the previous chapter tries to make clear, I finally conclude that he did not really have a method after all, at least not in the strong sense of the term. He did have a distinctive way of thinking and writing, that much is certain. But it was not one that can be nearly as readily systematized as his talk of philosophic method makes it seem.

Arthur Danto, an analytic philosopher of note, describes Dewey's way of writing as lacking in structure. "With Dewey," he says, "it's an unstructured world in which you sort of move through a fog" (Borradori, 1994, 90). His description, oddly enough, tallies quite well with the way

Dewey himself describes his philosophic journey, as we have seen in Chapter 4. He seldom does so publicly, however. Only in his poetry, which was not written for public consumption, do we come upon Dewey explicitly acknowledging the enveloping fog. To find it in his philosophical writing one must move beyond the confident talk about paths and maps that effectively hides it from view. As one does so, one gradually comes to realize that there are no paths or maps that tell one how to move from ordinary experience to the heights of abstraction (or vice versa). Nor is there a set of directions about how to forge such paths or construct such maps. Repeated encouragement plus a few general admonitions is about all one gets. As one begins to realize that nothing more definite than that will be forthcoming, the bank of fog that Danto mentioned rolls ominously into view on the horizon.

What I have just said is not meant to be harshly critical of Dewey, only mildly so. For if one reads him carefully enough, the warnings are there. Still, one has to say that they are not very well posted. He twice mentions the unusual candor that his method requires (LW1, 367, 369). I applaud him for that. But I still wish that his forthrightness extended to the difficulties that he himself experienced as a philosopher. Unfortunately, that aspect of his candor seems largely confined to his clandestine poetry, which is one reason I have drawn upon that poetry so heavily throughout this book.

Another way in which my view of Dewey changed during the writing of this book is that I came to see him as more firmly opposed to competing philosophical outlooks than I had previously realized. This change, which I discussed in some detail in the previous chapter, was due in part to my reading of John Shook's lucid exposition of Dewey's intellectual development as presented in his recent book, *Dewey's Empirical Theory of Knowledge and Reality* (2000). Shook's book, which did not appear until my work on this volume was almost complete, portrays with edifying clarity Dewey's early struggles to free himself from the dominance of absolute idealism, which was the reigning philosophic outlook during his early adulthood. It describes in detail the gradual evolution of Dewey's own philosophical perspective, tracing its metamorphosis through a concatenation of stages until it reaches the form of empirical naturalism that we find expounded in *Experience and Nature*. Shook's careful depiction of that history helped me to appreciate more fully than before not only the depth of Dewey's philosophic convictions (of which I was already aware) but also the care with which he presented his case in article after article and book after book, beginning during his days as a graduate student and continuing, as we have seen, until very near the end of his life. In Shook's telling of the story, the prize was seized upon fairly early in Dewey's career, albeit hard won from the start.

Did Dewey succeed in reaching his goal? Did he finally come upon a way of doing philosophy that satisfied his deepest yearnings? If not, was he at least getting there? Was the old would-be seafarer within sight of his destination toward the end of his life? His "hang and drift" remark certainly points in that direction. Yet, as I said in Chapter 4, I think it would be a mistake to give too facile a reading to that anecdote. It would be like adding a fairy-tale finish to a story that requires no such ending. For it is not that kind of story.

Dewey's search for a philosophic haven does not conform to the standard version of what the critic Harold Bloom called "a quest romance," although it does contain elements of that Romantic genre that Bloom so aptly named (1970, 5). It involves a quest, that much is certain. But to look upon it as a search for an elusive goal, pursued over a lifetime, as I was inclined to do at the start, is to miss a lot of what Dewey actually accomplished. For the happy truth about Dewey's life as a philosopher is that his search was far from directionless, nor did it go unrewarded until near the very end. Dewey knew where he was headed in the broadest of terms by mid-career, certainly long before he began writing *Experience and Nature*. This does not mean that he experienced nothing but smooth sailing from that point forward. On the contrary, even after he grew confident of his direction, he encountered difficulty. In fact, the going grew rougher than before in certain respects, as we have heard him testify. He found it harder to write, for one thing. Writing became difficult because he could no longer ignore the pressure of concrete experience. Instead of allowing intellectual themes to unfold dialectically, almost of their own accord, as he had become accustomed to doing, he had to adapt those intellectual habits to "the concrete diversity of experienced things" (LW5, 8). That adaptation did not come easy to Dewey, as complaints from readers, like Danto's quip about moving through a fog, attest. Yet he did push on, despite such difficulties. As he reported in 1939, the year he turned eighty,

> I have been engaged by means of published writings in developing the essentials of my present philosophical views for at least thirty-five years. . . . Inconsistencies and shifts have taken place; the most I can claim is that I have moved fairly steadily in one direction (LW14, 6).

"In one direction, was it? And in what direction was that, Mr. Dewey?" the inquisitive interrogator cannot help but inquire. Dewey turns away before answering, so we must answer for him, suppressing for now the impulse to insist that all talk about moving in this or that direction is only a figure of speech.

In the light of what was said above, just prior to Dewey's statement, one part of the answer to where he was headed has to be "Straight into the fog." But "into the fog" is not a direction. Or is it? It is so if we can imagine someone moving the other way. And, given what purportedly engendered that foggy condition for Dewey, to imagine the latter is not at all difficult. Moving away from the fog essentially means avoiding human entanglements. It means turning one's back on the problems that beset the bulk of humanity. It means playing it safe academically, asking the standard questions and using the approved procedures for answering them. To move in such a direction is certainly a way to go. In fact, it was precisely the direction that a growing number of Dewey's fellow philosophers were taking at the time. But it was not Dewey's way. He chose the opposite direction.

Though "straight into the fog" may constitute an answer of sorts to the question of where Dewey was headed for thirty-five years, it does not quite satisfy the condition of being a *straight* answer. It sounds evasive. What we still want to know is what lay beyond the fog for Dewey. Where was he headed in the long run?

But that is just the question that Heidegger's remark at the start of this Afterword warns us against asking. I am confident that Dewey would have issued the same warning. For he did not think in those terms. He had no ultimate destination toward which his philosophical labors were taking him. Indeed, even to imagine him headed toward such a terminus places him in the company of the philosophers with whom he most vehemently disagreed—those questing for certainty, those seeking a haven that lay beyond change, somewhere outside the boundary of human experience. For Dewey, there was no such resting place. There was only the struggle *within experience* to move on to regions of greater calm and comfort, not just material calm and physical comfort, of course, but social calm and psychological comfort as well.

Can one move in a fairly straight line without having an ultimate destination? Of course one can. People do it all the time. It is called trying to make life better for oneself and for others through an artful blend of thought, feeling, and action. Dewey managed to move in that general direction as a philosopher not just for thirty-five years but for far longer than that. What makes such a line straight rather than crooked? The relative constancy of the ideals propelling it, which in Dewey's case included his idealized conception of the philosopher's task. Can we learn from those ideals without following them blindly, which is to say, without treating Dewey as a philosophical signpost, a half-century-old scarecrow mutely pointing in but one direction? I am confident that we can—far more so now, I am pleased to say, than when this writing venture began.

Notes

INTRODUCTION

1. In the body of the text all references to Dewey's writings are keyed to *The Collected Works of John Dewey*, edited by Jo Ann Boydston and published by the Southern Illinois University Press. The abbreviations EW, MW, and LW, followed by specific volume and page numbers, stand for Early Works, 1882–1898; Middle Works, 1899–1924; and Later Works, 1925–1953, within that series of publications.

2. The original first chapter and the subsequent attempts to write introductions to the book's reissuance are reprinted as Appendices in Volume 1 of Dewey's Later Works.

3. My indebtedness to Shook's book is more fully acknowledged in the Afterword.

4. Readers interested in pursuing in greater depth any aspect of Dewey's thought have many choices available. The secondary literature is vast to begin with, and there has been a renewed surge of interest in Dewey's writings in recent years. A good place to start one's search through that literature is with the useful compilation of writings about Dewey recently prepared by Barbara Levine (1996). It covers the years 1886 to 1995. Three fairly recent collections of such scholarly writings have been edited by Hickman (1998), Garrison (1995), and Stuhr (1993).

Additionally, there has been a spate of book-length treatments of various aspects of Dewey's philosophy over the past two decades. Those I have found particularly valuable include Alexander (1987), Boisvert (1988), Burke (1994), Campbell (1995), Eldridge (1998), Hickman (1992), Shook (2000), Sleeper (1986), and Tiles (1990). A number of such book-length studies are especially directed to audiences of educators. These include Fishman and McCarthy (1998), Garrison (1997), Hansen (1995), Jackson (1998), and Tanner (1997). Three recent biographical studies of Dewey are those by Rockefeller (1991), Ryan (1995), and Westbrook (1991).

There has also been a renewed interest in pragmatism in general among philosophers. Those who show such an interest almost invariably take up

Dewey's ideas in some detail. Examples include Putnam (1992,1995), Rorty (1982), Seigfried (1996), and Shusterman (1992, 1997).

5. The lectures on which the book was based were initially presented before a joint meeting of the Eastern and Western Divisions of the American Philosophical Association in December 1922.

CHAPTER 1

1. The terms *philosophic method* and its close variant *philosophical method* appear in the titles of two of Dewey's very earliest writings. "Kant and Philosophic Method" was published in April 1884 (EW1, 34–47) and "Psychology as Philosophical Method" in January 1886 (EW1, 122–43).

Dewey often used paired terms, separated by "and," as the title of a book or chapter. Books of his with such titles include *School and Society* (MW1), *The Child and the Curriculum* (MW1), *Democracy and Education* (MW9), *The Public and Its Problems* (LW2), *Experience and Education* (LW13), *Philosophy and Civilization* (LW3, 5), *Freedom and Culture* (LW13), and, of course, the volume under discussion here (LW1).

2. For an excellent recent treatment of Dewey's intellectual development as it pertains to both absolute idealism and absolute realism, see Shook (2000).

3. The emergence of idealism and its place within the history of philosophy is obviously far more complex than this account allows. Nonetheless, the dynamics of its evolution as here outlined conforms roughly to the story of its emergence that Dewey gives.

4. The figurative language that Dewey draws upon here comprises a kind of leitmotif within his work as a whole. He often uses terms like "starting point," "direction," "objective," and "journey," to depict the philosopher's task. The significance of that travel imagery is a topic to which we shall return.

5. Hans Reichenbach, whose work in the philosophy of science exemplified those in the forefront of choosing the "other" route, explains the importance of mathematical training for philosophers in (of all places!) a volume honoring Dewey on his eightieth birthday.

In as much as modern physics in particular is intrinsically mathematical, philosophic analysis of modern science cannot be achieved without a profound study of mathematical methods. This is why in our time a qualified philosopher has to be a good mathematician—a maxim which our students of philosophy should note (1939, 191).

Reichenbach's use of the term "a qualified philosopher" (rather than, say, "a qualified philosopher of science") must have stung Dewey despite his age.

The term clearly implies that one lacking the required mathematical sophistication does not qualify as a philosopher "of our time." In replying to his critics, Dewey ignores that particular remark.

6. This line of reasoning is not Dewey's alone, needless to say. Indeed, more than one philospher over the years has thought that he himself has almost singlehandedly brought philosphy's project to its rational close. Among the moderns, Wittgenstein, following the completion of the *Tractatus* (1922), comes most readily to mind. Others, such as Richard Rorty, have credited various combinations of their fellow philosophers with having done the same; see Rorty (1979).

7. In his recent book on Dewey's political philosophy, Alan Ryan remarks on Dewey's skill in delivering "lay sermons," of which portions of this chapter of *Experience and Nature* might well serve as an example. He says: "The art was acquired by Dewey in his Sunday morning talks to the students at Michigan. Once he had the style, he never lost it" (1995, 366).

CHAPTER 2

1. It is statements like this, presumably, that have led a number of Dewey's readers to believe that he was out to substitute "science" for religion and for other more traditional sources of value. John E. Smith, for example, who otherwise writes quite sympathetically about Dewey's philosophy, claims that

> He seemed to think that somehow (one must say "somehow" because it is not clear exactly how) science is able to furnish all the standards of value and evaluation. In reply to his own question—"Where will regulation come from if we surrender familiar and traditionally prized values as our directive standards?"—Dewey answered, "Very largely from the findings of the natural sciences" (1963, 143).

Smith would be hard put, I believe, if pressed for a direct quotation to back that imagined answer. Nonetheless, from statements such as the one we have been considering here one can begin to understand how Smith and others might come to such a conclusion.

2. This is a crucial decision on Dewey's part, for it means, fundamentally, that he and his intellectual opponents will seldom if ever meet on level ground. They will remain, one might say, "methodologically estranged." The mathematically inclined empiricists, like Russell and members of the Vienna Circle, will be unable to wrestle Dewey to the ground because he is not willing to play by their rules, nor are they by his. As a result, the would-be opponents become mutually dismissive toward each other.

3. For what it is worth, I report that the sentence length in the revised chapter is markedly greater than in the original. The original averaged eight words per sentence, whereas the revision averages twenty-three. Since in sheer number of words overall the two versions are approximately equal in length (11,209 in the original, 12,720 in the revision), this means that the revised version also has far fewer sentences (586, compared with 1380 in the original). If sentence length is positively correlated with difficulty, a reasonable if somewhat dubious assumption, this would mean that the revised version is noticeably more difficult than the original. I can only report that such a difference was not evident to me during my own reading of the two versions.

CHAPTER 3

1. He divides the texts into fourteen sections, indicated by roman numerals. I cannot believe that Dewey would himself have indicated such divisions.

2. For readers who would prefer making their own judgment about the worth of the information in that table showing the frequency of key words and phrases, see Table 3.1.

3. I think, for example, of the recent writings of Richard Shweder and other anthropologists of like mind. See Stigler, Shweder, and Herdt (Eds), *Cultural Psychology*, 1990.

4. This is not to say that philosophers lack all interest in cultures other than their own. Dewey, in fact, had many such interests. He traveled to Turkey and Russia. He spent more than two years in Japan and China during the period between 1919 and 1921. Moreover, his stay in China, Dewey wrote to a friend, was the "most interesting and intellectually the most profitable thing I've ever done" (quoted in Dykhuizen, 1973, 205). Yet even while Dewey was overseas his mission was not to study Chinese or Japanese culture. It was to bring the fruits of his own form of philosophizing to foreign shores. He did so quite successfully, incidentally, lecturing to scores of eager audiences in China and an appreciable number in Japan as well.

CHAPTER 4

1. These only came to light after his death. For the story of Dewey's poems and how they were discovered, see the Introduction by Jo Ann Boydston in John Dewey, *The Poems of John Dewey*, 1977.

2. Not all of Dewey's metaphorical sailors are that lucky. One of the most poignant of his "nautical" poems begins:

Table 3.1. Frequency of Key Words and Phrases in Original, Revised, and Unfinished Versions of Chapter 1.

Word or Phrase	Original Version	Revised Version	Unfinished Introduction
Experience	142	209	29
Ordinary (ordinary experience)	0	16	0
Primary experience	0	23	0
Nature	17	54	41
Philosophy	27	50	48
Empirical method	18	33	0
Science	24	14	55
Denote	16	5	0
Denotation (denotative method)	12	2	0
Reflective analysis	0	4	0
Reflective	0	18	7
Reflection	19	28	15
Culture (cultural)	0	0	11
Human	9	13	41

> *The rope is cut, the anchor falls*
> *And is left alone in the mud,*
> *Submerged.*

and ends:

> *Drifts the ship. The rope end, cut,*
> *Flaps upon the side and knocks,*
> *Knocks. You can hear it through the*
> *blowing wind,*
> *And through the screeching of the sails*
> *On the masts.*

And when I cannot hear it I know
It flaps and knocks
All the time.
(1977, 43–44)

3. Wittgenstein would be my nominee for the twentieth-century philosopher who comes closest to using the mapmaker imagery naturally. He does so in *Philosophical Investigations* (1958) with his talk of "perspicuous representation." In PI122 he says, "A main source of our failure to understand is that we do not *command a clear view* of the use of our words. . . . The concept of a perspicuous representation [übersichtliche Darstellung] is of fundamental significance for us. It earmarks the form of account we give, the way we look at things."

4. Cavell calls this natural figurative use of language "projecting a word." He says, "The phenomenon I am calling 'projecting a word' is the fact of language which, I take it, is sometimes responded to by saying that 'All language is metaphorical'" (1979, 190).

5. I say "close to" because it is not entirely clear to me that philosophy traffics in abstractions more than does mathematics, let's say, or theology.

6. For a very different take on Dewey's use of the mapmaking imagery, see the article by Richard Boisvert (1998). In an argument whose moves are far too subtle to summarize here, Boisvert takes Dewey to task for not being more explicit in his formulations of his own metaphysical position. He advises passing over Dewey's comments about the importance of identifying "generic traits" as a kind of metaphysical exercise. He recommends instead paying special attention to Dewey's efforts to articulate "paradigmatic instances of the real" (p. 159). Boisvert's nominees for that designation are "events" and "the social."

Boisvert calls for a better way of staking out Dewey's distinctive position than is afforded by "his approach via generic traits" (p. 159). I see this as being somewhat similar to my wish to see Dewey's approach to philosophy more fully portrayed than one finds it in Dewey's talk about "philosophic method."

7. There is evidence in Dewey's poetry that he looked upon America in similar, Romantic terms. In a poem titled "The New World—," he writes

Of a sudden a blazing star
Ruddier than heart of flowing gold
Swept from out the vastness of the night,
The distant boundless eastern night
As the heaven filled with strange splendor,
The world, wearied with the weight
Of its tamed courses, pauses, startled
By the adventure of a soul

Whose only chart through untracked spaces
Was faith in the miracles courage works
Even in the timidities of custom,
 . . .
And now it plunges into darkness,
The darkness of the unknown,
The unforeseeable, the untried.
Alone it goes. . . .
(1977, 58)

CHAPTER 5

1. See, for example, Smith (1963). Summarizing Dewey's supposed adulation of science, Smith concludes, "One of the most reliable clues to the true status of science in American culture is the strength of the belief that science can be made to do in one stroke the work traditionally performed by ethics and religion. Dewey shared that belief" (p. 150).

2. One of the things that may get in the way of our thinking about the overlap of science and philosophy in these terms (perhaps it got in Dewey's way as well) is the stereotype (the mental picture) of the white-coated scientist fiddling away in her laboratory amidst a jumble of flasks and vials and other pieces of equipment. To learn from the scientist, that picture informs, is to do *what* she does, not *as* she does. But that can't be the whole of it, because we certainly do not expect the philosopher (or any other investigator save the scientist) to be fiddling around in a maze of physical equipment. What is it, then, that causes the comparison to misfire? It must be what we read into that stereotypic picture. And what is that? My guess is that it has to do with an imbalance of *things* over *ideas*, of *action* over *thought*. Here too we seem to be misled by a picture.

3. This personal transformation is lucidly traced in Shook (2000).

4. Figures such as Josiah Royce, Thomas Hill Green, and George Santayana. For a concise history of idealism in American philosophy see Schneider (1963).

5. The latter included principally Bertrand Russell and his followers in England, plus those European and American philosophers associated with logical positivism and its philosophical offshoots. For a recent overview of that movement see Stroll (2000).

6. Dewey had a special epithet that he applied to all means of trying to escape from experience. He called them instances of "the philosophical fallacy." What they had in common, as he described it, was "the conversion of eventual functions into antecedent existence" (LW1, 34). This meant taking some product of logical analysis and treating it as though it had existence prior to

the analysis itself, that is, as though it lay outside experience. It mattered not to Dewey whether that maneuver was performed "in behalf of mathematical substances, esthetic essences, the purely physical order of nature, or God" (LW1, 34). Its fallacious character remained the same.

7. Dewey was far more a social activist than were most university professors of his day. His somewhat low opinion of the quietism of the average professor is revealed in a remark he made in calling for a revival of interest in Plato. Such a return would be, he said,

> back to the Plato whose highest flight of metaphysics always terminated with a social and practical turn, and not to the artificial Plato constructed by unimaginative commentators who treat him as the original university professor (LW5, 155).

8. In his intriguing study, *Dewey and Eros*, Jim Garrison proposes that Dewey held to "a consistent, although constrained, philosophy of love that laced together the threads of his educational thinking." Indeed, Garrison goes on to claim that "It is not possible to comprehend his philosophy of education without appreciating his hidden philosophy of love" (1997, xx).

I am not sure how to make Garrision's thesis jibe with my own sense of Dewey's strong antipathies toward philosophical positions contrary to his own. Perhaps the two perspectives are far more commensurable than they first appear. What Garrison is calling Dewey's "philosophy of love" may be quite harmonious with what I prefer to think of as his wholehearted acceptance of life's complexities. Dewey's own term for his attitude in the face of that abundance is one that is usually associated with religious devotion and therefore might be looked upon as a form of love. He calls it piety.

9. That principle, incidentally, epitomizes Dewey's commitment to empiricism. It is, in effect, his "No Exit" sign.

References

Alexander, Thomas M. 1987. *John Dewey's Theory of Art, Experience, and Nature: The Horizons of Feeling*. Albany: State University of New York Press.

Bloom, Harold, editor. 1970. *Romanticism and Consciousness: Essays in Criticism*. New York: W. W. Norton & Company.

Boisvert, Raymond D. 1988. *Dewey's Metaphysics*. New York: Fordam University Press.

Boisvert, Richard. 1998. "Dewey's Metaphysics: Ground-Map of the Prototypically Real." In *Reading Dewey*, edited by Larry A. Hickman, 149–65. Bloomington: Indiana University Press.

Borradori, Giovanna. 1994. *The American Philosopher*. Chicago: University of Chicago Press.

Burke, Tom. 1994. *Dewey's New Logic: A Reply to Russell*. Chicago: University of Chicago Press.

Campbell, James. 1995. *Understanding John Dewey*. Chicago: Open Court Publishing Company.

Cavell, Stanley. 1979. *The Claim of Reason*. New York: Oxford University Press.

———. 1984. *Themes Out of School: Effects and Causes*. Chicago: University of Chicago Press.

———. 1989. *This New Yet Unapproachable America*. Albuquerque, New Mexico: Living Batch Press.

Dewey, John. 1977. *The Poems of John Dewey*. Edited by Jo Ann Boydston. Carbondale: Southern Illinois University Press.

Dykhuizen, George. 1973. *The Life and Mind of John Dewey*. Carbondale: Southern Illinois University Press.

Eldridge, Michael. 1998. *Transforming Experience: John Dewey's Cultural Instrumentalism*. Nashville: Vanderbilt University Press.

Fishman, Stephen M., and Lucille McCarthy. 1998. *John Dewey and the Challenge of Classroom Practice*. New York: Teachers College Press.

Garrison, Jim. 1995. *The New Scholarship on Dewey*. Boston: Kluwer Academic Publishers.

———. 1997. *Dewey and Eros*. New York: Teachers College Press.

Geertz, Clifford. 2000. *Available Light: Anthropological Reflections on Philosophical Topics*. Princeton: Princeton University Press.

Goethe, Johann Wolfgang, von. 1987. *From My Life: Poetry and Truth*. Edited by Thomas Saine and Jeffrey L. Sammons and translated by Robert R. Heitner. New York: Suhrkamp.

Hansen, David T. 1995. *The Call to Teach*. New York: Teachers College Press.

Heidegger, Martin. 1962. *Being and Time*. Translated by John Macquarrie and Edmund Robinson. New York: Harper and Row.

———. 1968. *What is Called Thinking?* New York: Harper & Row.

———. 1987. *An Introduction to Metaphysics*. New Haven, Connecticut: Yale University Press.

———. 1998. "Letter on 'Humanism'." In *Pathmarks*, edited by William McNeill, 239–76. New York: Cambridge University Press.

Hickman, Larry A. 1992. *John Dewey's Pragmatic Technology*. Bloomington: Indiana University Press.

———, editor. 1998. *Reading Dewey*. Bloomington: Indiana University Press.

Jackson, Philip W. 1998. *John Dewey and the Lessons of Art*. New Haven, Connecticut: Yale University Press.

Kant, Immanuel. 1952. *The Critique of Pure Reason*. Translated by J. M. D. Meiklejohn, 1–250. Chicago: Encyclopedia Britannica.

Levine, Barbara, editor. 1996. *Works About John Dewey: 1886–1995*. Carbondale: Southern Illinois University Press.

Malinowski, Bronislaw. 1937. "Culture." In *Encyclopaedia of the Social Sciences*, edited by Alvin Johnson, 621–23. New York: Macmillan.

Morgenbesser, Sidney, editor. 1977. *Dewey and His Critics*. Essays from the Journal of Philosophy. New York: The Journal of Philosophy, Inc.

Putnam, Hillary. 1992. *Renewing Philosophy*. Cambridge, Massachusetts: Harvard University Press.

———. 1995. *Pragmatism*. Cambridge, Massachusetts: Blackwell.

Quine, Willard Van, Orman. 1980. *From a Logical Point of View*. Cambridge, Massachusetts: Harvard University Press.

Reichenbach, Hans. 1939. "Dewey's Theory of Science." In *The Philosophy of John Dewey*, edited by Paul Arthur Schilpp, 157–92. New York: Tudor Publishing Company.

Rockefeller, Steven C. 1991. *John Dewey: Religious Faith and Democratic Humanism*. New York: Columbia University Press.

Rorty, Richard. 1979. *Philosophy and the Mirror of Nature*. Princeton: Princeton University Press.

———. 1982. *Consequences of Pragmatism*. Minneapolis: University of Minnesota Press.

Ryan, Alan. 1995. *John Dewey and the High Tide of American Liberalism*. New York: W. W. Norton & Company.

Schilpp, Paul Arthur, editor. 1939. *The Philosophy of John Dewey*. New York: Tudor Publishing Company.

Schneider, Herbert W. 1963. *A History of American Philosophy*. New York: Columbia University Press.

Seigfried, Charlene Haddock. 1996. *Pragmatism and Feminism*. Chicago: University of Chicago Press.

Sellars, Wilfrid. 1996. *Naturalism and Ontology*. Atascadero, California: Ridgeview Publishing Company.

———. 1997. *Empiricism and the Philosophy of Mind*. Cambridge, Massachusetts: Harvard University Press.

Shook, John R. 2000. *Dewey's Empirical Theory of Knowledge and Reality*. Nashville: Vanderbilt University Press.

Shusterman, Richard. 1992. *Pragmatist Aesthetics: Living Beauty, Rethinking Art*. Cambridge, Massachusetts: Blackwell.

———. 1997. *Practicing Philosophy: Pragmatism and the Philosophical Life*. New York: Routledge.

Sleeper, R. W. 1986. *The Necessity of Pragmatism*. New Haven, Connecticut: Yale University Press.

Smith, John E. 1963. *The Spirit of American Philosophy*. New York: Oxford University Press.

Stevens, Wallace. 1990a. *Opus Posthumous: Poems, Plays, Prose*. Edited by Milton J. Bates. New York: Vintage Books.

———. 1990b. *The Palm at the End of the Mind: Selected Poems and a Play*. New York: Vintage Books.

Stigler, James W., Richard A. Shweder, and Gilbert Herdt, editors. 1990. *Cultural Psychology: Essays on Comparative Human Development*. New York: Cambridge University Press.

Stroll, Avrum. 2000. *Twentieth-Century Analytic Philosophy*. New York: Columbia University Press.

Stuhr, John J., editor. 1993. *Philosophy and the Reconstruction of Culture: Pragmatic Essays After Dewey*. Albany: State University of New York Press.

Tanner, Laurel. 1997. *Dewey's Laboratory School: Lessons for Today*. New York: Teachers College Press.

Tiles, J. E. 1990. *Dewey*. New York: Routledge.

Westbrook, Robert B. 1991. *John Dewey and American Democracy*. Ithaca, New York: Cornell University Press.

Wittgenstein, Ludwig. 1922. *Tractatus Logico-Philosophicus*. New York: Humanities Press.

———. 1958. *Philosophical Investigations*. Edited by G. E. M. Anscombe and R. Rhees and translated by G. E. M. Anscombe. Oxford, England: Blackwell.

Index

Absolute idealism, 5–8, 31, 65
  See also Idealism
Absolute realism, 7, 8, 65
Acton, Lord, 45, 48, 53
Alexander, Thomas M., 103, 111*n*
Anthropology, as akin to
  philosophy, 52, 54, 96
Arnold, Matthew, 52

Bloom, Harold, 100, 111*n*
Boisvert, Richard, 103, 108, 111*n*
Borradori, Giovanna, 77, 83, 84, 98,
  111*n*
Boydston, Jo Ann, 103, 106, 111*n*
Burke, Tom, 103, 111*n*

Campbell, James, 103, 111*n*
Carnap, Rudolph, 58
Cavell, Stanley, 24, 108, 111*n*
  criticism of Dewey, 77, 80–81, 83–
  84, 89, 98

Danto, Arthur, critical of Dewey's
  way of writing, 98–100
Davidson, Donald, 20
Denotation, 15–19, 42
Denotative method, 35
Dewey, John
  autobiographical statement, 87
  founding of Laboratory School,
  85
  impatience with non-empirical
  philosophers, 37, 39

nautical imagery of, 59, 73–76
reply to Max Otto, 22
three philosophical commitments
  of, 59
See also Experience and Nature,
  publishing history of
Dialectical reasoning, Dewey's
  rejection of , 10, 11
Dykhuizen, George, 106, 111*n*

Eldridge, Michael, 103, 111*n*
Empirical method, 3–4, 6, 14, 16, 32
Empirical naturalism, as one of
  Dewey's name for his form of
  philosophy, 26–30
  See also Naturalistic empiricism;
  Naturalistic humanism
Experience
  as all-inclusive, 15
  distinctive features and trends, 13
  faith in, 28, 40, 50, 55, 60
  forms of, 9–10, 12–13
  as method, 16, 19
  as Protean, 10, 69
  subjective aspects of, 5, 6, 8
  two ways of thinking about, 4
Experience and Nature
  initial first chapter, overview, 1–
  23
  1925 Preface and revised first
  chapter, overview, 24–40
  proposed change of title, 51
  publishing history of, xvi–xvii

About the Author

Philip W. Jackson is the David Lee Shillinglaw Distinguished Service Professor Emeritus in the Departments of Education and Psychology at the University of Chicago. He holds a Ph.D. from Teachers College, Columbia University. He is a past President of the John Dewey Society and the American Educational Research Association. In addition to *John Dewey and the Philosopher's Task*, he is the author of *Life in Classrooms* (1968), *The Practice of Teaching* (1986), *Untaught Lessons* (1992), and *John Dewey and the Lessons of Art* (1998), Dr. Jackson also co-authored *Creativity and Intelligence* (with J. W. Getzels, 1962), and *The Moral Life of Schools* (with R. Boostrom and D. Hansen, 1993).